THE Shuttleworth COLLECTION

D1379197

Shuttleworth

THE HISTORIC AEROPLANES

DAVID OGILVY

Airlife
England

The Founder: Richard Shuttleworth.

Copyright © David Ogilvy 1989, 1994

First published 1989
Revised edition first published 1994
by Airlife Publishing Ltd.

ISBN 1 85310 499 X Case Bound
ISBN 1 85310 503 1 Paperback

All rights reserved. No part of this book may be reproduced
or transmitted in any form or by any means, electronic or
mechanical including photocopying, recording or by any
information storage and retrieval system, without permission
from the Publisher in writing.

Printed in Singapore
by Kyodo Printing Co (S'pore) Pte Ltd.

Airlife Publishing Ltd.

101 Longden Road, Shrewsbury SY3 9EB

Half Title Page:

The 1924 DH 51.

Title Page:

The 1935 Gloster Gladiator.

Introduction

I am very pleased to be able to bring up-to-date the story of the Shuttleworth Collection at a time when the Shuttleworth Trust attains its fiftieth anniversary in 1994. The Collection itself, though, goes back a further 16 years, for as long ago as 1928 Richard Ormonde Shuttleworth – the founder – acquired his first collector's piece. This was a Panhard Levassor car, then almost thirty years old, which remains at Old Warden today and, still retained in full working order, is close to reaching its 100th year. Much, though, has happened in the 66 years since it all began and my aim here is to bring the story to life. For 'life' is what the Collection is all about. It is not a 'dead' static museum, for although there are numerous items and artefacts that remain in their display spaces, almost all the main mechanical items – aeroplanes and road vehicles – are brought out regularly for all to see, to hear and to appreciate in action. Here I aim to tell you something about them all.

Today the Shuttleworth Collection is unique. It is the world's only permanent exhibition of *flyable* historic aeroplanes dating from the birth of powered flight and

The Collection's 1941 Spitfire Mk Vc.

extending into World War II, all in the appropriate setting of a small, all-grass rural aerodrome. People come from literally all over the world for the experience, but to appreciate the depth of detail involved, visitors need some guidance; this is the purpose of the book that you have now in your hands.

The first printed guide book appeared in 1964, by which time the Collection was thirty-six years into its existence. However, in the earlier period, the gates were not open regularly to the public, but over the past thirty years since the start of daily opening, the range of exhibits has expanded and the way in which they are displayed has been made more visitor-friendly. Many of the changes are described in this book, in which I try not only to express the scenes and atmosphere of the past but to look into the visions for the years leading into the twenty-first century.

Action is the keynote. On one day you may visit Old Warden and study the exhibits in the relative quiet of mid-week, but you may come again on a busy summer Sunday on which the small, timeless, all-grass aerodrome is abuzz with activity. Imagine a line-up of genuine early veteran aeroplanes, with a Bleriot of 1909 that is identical to the machine which made the first aerial crossing of the English Channel in that year, and the Blackburn mono-plane that first flew from the sands at Filey in Yorkshire in 1912, now the oldest original British aeroplane that flies anywhere in the world, ready to take their turns at the end of the day; a trio of de Havilland Moths of the twenties and thirties taxying out to the take-off point for flypasts into nostalgia, and, on a more serious note, the only airworthy specimens of the Hawker Hind light bomber and Gloster Gladiator fighter performing in the air together, representing types in service with the Royal Air Force in the years just before the outbreak of war in 1939. All this progress, though, from the first manned powered flight, has happened within a human lifetime, for some people alive today were born before the aeroplane became a practical proposition.

This very special story — not just about the Shuttleworth Collection but about the development of aviation — can be presented in many ways, but as it happens at Old Warden and nowhere else in the world, we must place it all into proper perspective, giving words to the historical and technical aspects and showing the action in pictures — in colour. For although the Shuttleworth Collection is a museum, it is much more. It is the story of the *flying* machine and *working* road vehicle. That is why the illustrations in this new book are concentrated on 'living' views, for that is what the place is all about.

Right: The Hawker Hind and Gloster Gladiator ready to taxi for a display.

When we see Old Warden today or read about its present activities and future plans, we must not forget the reason behind our good fortune. One man — Richard Ormonde Shuttleworth — possessed the foresight to start acquiring, first, early cars and, later, veteran aeroplanes; his aim was not to have them as static exhibits, but as items of machinery that must be made to work as well as they had done when they were built. Without his early efforts there would be no base on which the present range of exhibits could have been built.

Now in the mid-nineties the work continues towards the needs for the next century, with extended facilities for visitors and always with several restoration projects under way.

I have the good fortune to bring to this book a considerable amount of information and detail that relate to first-hand experience of the Collection's work. I was lucky enough to have 25 years closely connected with Old Warden, with 14 as General Manager and a further eleven in a consultancy capacity, with especial responsibility for the displays and aerodrome activity generally. Throughout this time I had the privilege of flying many of the historic aeroplanes. All this has been of considerable practical value when putting together the various sections of the Shuttleworth story, but it would not have been complete or wholly accurate without help from many others. Peter Symes, the General Manager, has provided information about recent changes to the Collection's constitution. For much technical detail, we must all be especially grateful for the material provided by Bob Elliott, the Librarian, and Chris Morris, the Chief Engineer. Unfortunately I cannot thank by name every person who has provided information, for this has come from numerous sources, but I mention Owen Dinsdale for his update on the Sea Hurricane. For most of the original pictures credit must go to Michael Vines of Photo Link who has been taking photographs at Old Warden for almost as many years as I can remember! For recent photographs, I am very grateful to Steven Jefferson of the Aviation Picture Library who has provided several 'atmosphere' pictures of the Collection's activities. For some of the car photographs, though, I wish to thank Michael Ware who took them in his capacity as curator of the National Motor Museum, to which body I am indebted for permission to publish. Finally, a book of this nature fails to come together as a meaningful guide without some organisational effort and, in this context, Karen Ward of the Collection's staff has not only typed the text but has carried out many essential administrative tasks.

I hope that you will gain plenty of information and pleasure from this book, which differs noticeably from its predecessor – *Shuttleworth: the Historic Aeroplanes* – in its expansion to include wider and more detailed coverage of the important road vehicles with which it all started.

DAVID OGILVY

Right: Replica of the 1910 Bristol Boxkite.

1
The Shuttleworth Collection: Origins

The Shuttleworth name goes back in aviation history considerably further than the year in which the Collection was started. In 1842 the firm of Clayton and Shuttleworth was founded in Lincoln, originally to supply iron water pipes and, from only three years later, portable steam engines, of which the company had built ten thousand by 1870. In the following years, threshing engines were produced in vast numbers and machines to Clayton and Shuttleworth design were manufactured not only in Lincoln, but also in Vienna and Budapest. A few of the early steam-powered products remain in existence today, as preserved veterans whose proud owners show them to the public at various rallies.

Although most of these were road engines, the company built some railway rolling stock and a few steam loco-motives for the London and North Eastern Railway. However, it was during the First World War that aircraft came into the Shuttleworth scene. In 1916 the firm made tail stabilizers and gondola parts for submarine scout airships that were used by the Admiralty for coastal patrol duties, but later in the same year Sopwith Triplanes were built for the Royal Naval Air Service and fifty were produced in the Lincoln works. During this time a Sopwith Camel N 5420 was sent to the Company to use as a pattern aircraft and, subsequently, between 1917 and 1919, more than five hundred Camels were built in the company's Titanic Works. These machines — and the Triplanes — were taken to Robey's aerodrome at nearby Bracebridge Heath for final assembly, air testing and delivery.

One Shuttleworth-built Camel, B 7270, on the strength of No 209 Squadron and flown by Captain R Brown, is officially recorded as shooting down the famous German ace Captain (Baron) Manfred von Richthofen; after the war, to mark this, a souvenir leaflet was published by Clayton and Shuttleworth. One Lincoln-built Camel, B 5747, which served with the Belgian Air Service, remains in existence today and is on display in Brussels Air Museum.

During the war, a new (third) factory was constructed. This was alongside the River Witham. Here the company built forty-six of the large Handley Page 0/400 twin-engine bombers powered by Rolls-Royce Eagles. Too massive to transport by road, these were flown out of a small field adjacent to the works from which, lightly loaded, they flew the short distance to a nearby Aircraft Acceptance Park. In May 1918 contracts were placed for the production of 150 Vickers Vimy heavy bomber/transports, but only one was completed before the end of the war which removed the requirement for these machines.

In the twenties and thirties relatively few people thought about obtaining early cars or aeroplanes, but Richard Shuttleworth had the foresight and determination to obtain some exceptionally worthwhile examples of both. The fortunate son of a wealthy land-owning family, he had access to the space necessary to build workshops, a hangar and the small grass aerodrome at Old Warden, near Biggleswade in Bedfordshire. Perhaps the aero-drome is one of the most significant aspects of it all, for Richard was no museum man; he obtained items to make them work. His cars participated in the annual Brighton runs and his aeroplanes flew regularly at displays.

Today the name Shuttleworth is known to many thou-sands of people all over the world, but in view of the Collection's long existence this is not surprising.

In September 1988, a special sixtieth anniversary pageant enabled discerning visitors to see the scale of the operation that had been established. Although historically a very special event, this pageant was one of the regular series of displays held at Old Warden throughout the summer months. But it was not always like this, for there has been a steady growth since 1928, when Richard Shuttleworth began his collecting activities by acquiring a (then) twenty-eight-year-old Panhard Levassor motor car. That car remains a key exhibit today and is in excellent running order.

Although, through the Collection, Richard Shuttleworth is remembered mainly for his avid acquisition of historic aircraft and vehicles, we must not overlook his activities as a successful racing driver; he based his racing operations on the famous track at Brooklands, where he had his original workshop, but he participated in events in many parts of the continent and even as far afield as South Africa, where on 1 January 1936 he had a serious accident that ended his racing career. It was at Brooklands, significantly, that in 1932 he bought his first aeroplane; not then a collector's piece, but a four-year-old de Havilland Moth that he used as his regular fly-about, particularly for journeys between there and Old Warden. With the passage of time, that Moth has gained in rarity value to become one of the leading items on show; as evidence of the years that have gone, this Moth has lived on one aerodrome for longer than any other aeroplane in the history of aviation!

In addition to collecting and racing, Richard Shuttleworth founded the Warden Aviation Company, based at Heston and equipped with three Desoutters and a DH Dragon for charter flying; the Dragon was specially modified with a Carden-Ford engine as a generator and the aircraft was fitted with an array of lights for aerial advertising at night. Several companies, including two breweries, placed contracts, but the authorities of the time reacted to unfavourable public opinion and the project was banned almost before it had begun, so the not-in-my-backyard (NIMBY) syndrome had started even then. As a Director of Pobjoy Airmotor and later of the Comper Aircraft Co Ltd of Hooton Park, Cheshire, Richard flew a diminutive single-seat Swift to India on a marketing tour. His aeronautical activities at Old Warden were mainly on the technical side and these were carried out in the name of the Warden Engineering Company, based in the one hangar near the aerodrome gate, above which were his drawing office and associated rooms; today that hangar houses the engineering workshops, while the upstairs area is the Collection's main office block housing the administrative staff. Early in these proceedings L A Jackson had come from Brooklands to Old Warden as the first engineer; apart from war service in the Royal Air Force, during which he became a Squadron Leader in the Engineering Branch, Tony ('Jacko') Jackson remained with the Collection until he retired as Manager in 1966.

All the Old Warden activities stopped on the outbreak of war in 1939; the aircraft, vehicles and supporting items were stored wherever space could be found to house them; Richard joined the Royal Air Force to qualify as a Service pilot, but unfortunately he was killed in a flying accident in a Fairey Battle light bomber in 1940. The buildings and aerodrome were used for dismantling, assembling and flight-testing of various light types then in RAF use; these included Proctors, Harvards and Magisters, on which extensive maintenance and repair work was carried out on the airframe components in premises in Biggleswade owned by Owen Godfrey Ltd and Mantles Garages Ltd. The activities at the airfield, which included engine overhaul, were carried out through staff employed by Shrager Brothers Ltd, who formed their own Home Guard platoon to protect the premises. A second hangar and several smaller buildings were erected during this time and the maintenance flight testing was carried out by a Service pilot detached from the nearby Royal Air Force station at Henlow.

In April 1944 Mrs Dorothy Shuttleworth founded and endowed the Richard Ormonde Shuttleworth Remembrance Trust in her son's memory for 'the promotion of education and training in the science practice and history of aviation and automotive transport by the provision of a collection of aircraft and other appropriate objects for exhibition to the public and in the science and practice of

The very start of the Shuttleworth Collection in 1928: the 1900 Panhard Levassor.

Overleaf: The 1917 Bristol Fighter in its earlier markings.

agriculture by the provision and conduct of a college'.

The latter subject is managed by Shuttleworth College, part of Cranfield University since 1988, centred upon the Victorian house built on Old Warden Park in 1872 by Joseph Shuttleworth, while the aims of the Collection are carried out on the 33 acre site of Old Warden Aerodrome. Until April 1993 the Shuttleworth Collection carried on trading under the historical title of Warden Aviation and Engineering. Then, following the Charities Act 1992 it was incorporated as a private limited company as a preliminary to the conversion of the Richard Shuttleworth Remembrance Trust as a whole to a Trust Corporation re-titled the Shuttleworth Trust in November 1993.

The educational aspect of the Collection's activities must not be overlooked; students of all ages and from all over the world use Old Warden for their historical studies and researches; many thousands of schoolchildren visit the Collection each year to be given explanatory talks

about the background of aviation and transport and to see the products of the past; lectures are given over a wide geographical area to specialist clubs and societies wishing to learn about the early stages of development of the flying machine; and there are several Shuttleworth publications.

To support all this is an ever-growing range of working items that are on static view daily and which can be seen in action on special occasions. Much remains to be done, for the Collection is financed from its own gate receipts and shop sales; this calls for a tight working budget, so limitations of space, workshop capacity, availability of the skilled workforce and other enforced constraints must mean that many tasks wait for several years in the queue before they can be tackled. At present the ruling policy lays main stress on restoring and maintaining the most significant historic aeroplanes, with a separate but smaller department giving similar treatment to selected early road vehicles. A point that many people forget is that a working technical object, once restored, needs constant running maintenance, so each completed item presents a permanent work commitment and therefore reduces the capacity available for further restoration.

As the tasks increase in scope and complexity, so must the supporting facilities. In the seventies two new hangars and workshops were built and by 1979 engine and machine shops and bonded stores had been constructed within the existing buildings; in 1980, a new hangar was opened to public viewing to provide space for a significant increase in displayed material. In 1982, though, a departure from previous policy reached fruition, when a new display building was completed especially to house aeroplanes of de Havilland origin. Now, with more space available, extensive effort is being devoted to improving the presentation of the static exhibits.

To provide a capability for operating heavier and faster aircraft there have been three physical expansions to the aircraft manoeuvring area of the aerodrome, but still this retains the essential timelessness of a smallish all-grass aerodrome in a rural area. The grass surface and availability of several take-off and landing directions are critical for the early aircraft, many of which would be unable to operate from today's airfields with single hard runways.

The Collection's normal routine activity should be self-supporting; however, this cannot cover the costs of the major projects, such as a particularly expensive restoration task or the provision of a new hangar in which to display the exhibits when they have been restored. For such purposes specialized appeals may be launched, while financial help is always welcome; money can be donated for a specific purpose or, more usually, for the overall good of the whole Collection. Help in kind, too, plays its part, with many organizations and individuals providing services free or at drastically reduced prices; only with such constant support from outside can the work be continued at its present encouraging pace.

A way in which many people show their support for the cause is by joining the Shuttleworth Veteran Aeroplane Society; in return, members receive special entry privileges and are kept in contact with plans and progress through regular news circulars. Membership, which spreads well into four figures, includes historians, enthusiasts and other supporters from almost every country in the world. The benefits are mutual.

To keep overheads pruned, the staff members are kept to a practical minimum, but there are countless duties to be performed; aircraft and vehicle restoration and maintenance, library and research work, sales activities, party visits, building and aerodrome maintenance, accounts, promotion and publicity, general administration and heavy daily correspondence, dealing with inquiries and the planning, operation and management of a well-loaded events programme are some. But how many visitors, perhaps, realize that the international promotion/ publicity programme with its preparation, printing and circulation must go ahead energetically throughout the darkest winter months each year? Or that when a historic aeroplane is dismantled for full restoration, this may be the start of a task that will take five or more years? Or that the same machine will need extensive reconditioning again about ten years after it emerges for the first time? Or that initial preparations for a large flying display must begin nearly a year ahead of the date of the event?

The Collection is very much alive throughout the year; alive to the changes that are taking place everywhere, but equally aware of the need to retain that special informal dateless atmosphere which means so much to so many; alive in that the items in its care are not static museum exhibits, but working examples of some of the best of the past; alive, too, to the responsibilities that go with that — whether testing a steam car with an eighty-years-old boiler, or maintaining or flying the last surviving specimen of a famous historic aeroplane. Although different times of the year produce changes in the nature of the work, there is no slack season at Shuttleworth. There is always more than enough to do; and plenty to see.

In this book I aim to describe the aeroplanes, the road vehicles and some of the associated items in a sequence and manner that explain their development; you can work straight through as though reading a novel (which it is not!), or select the sections to satisfy your own quest for information, or just absorb the life and atmosphere of the Collection from the many full-colour illustrations; but first turn over to see how it all began.

2
Development of
the Flying Machine

The Pioneers

The brothers Wilbur and Orville Wright must take full credit for the first man-carrying powered flights, starting with the famous 'straights' flown at Kittyhawk, North Carolina, USA, on 17 December 1903, but there were pioneers before them who very nearly succeeded.

Few will doubt that Sir George Cayley was the person who started aviation in its modern sense. He gained a great knowledge of aerodynamics, even to the extent of proving that on a cambered aerofoil more lift is generated by the reduced pressure on the upper surface than from the increased pressure beneath; from 1804 he was flying machines of various shapes and sizes with equally varying levels of success. The theoretical knowledge required to produce sustained flight was there, but for about a hundred years the lack of a suitable engine prevented any real achievement in the way of powered flight. There were many imaginative ideas, of which Henson's 'Aerial Steam Carriage' of 1842 became perhaps the best known, but although the design incorporated many novel ideas that bore future fruit for others, it remained only a paper exercise.

Because of problems of power — or lack of it — experiments with gliding played a lead part in the development of flight, particularly over matters of control-lability in the air. No one could equal the pioneering efforts of the German Otto Lilienthal, who flew successfully from 1891 onwards; in fact, development has turned a full circle, for he hung beneath his machine, shifting his body and legs to move the centre of gravity and therefore achieving limited manoeuvrability in broadly the manner used today by the modern weight-shift microlight and hang-glider. To achieve positive control response more rapidly, Lilienthal experimented later with more conven-tial control surfaces, but he was killed in 1896 before he had developed these. Nearer home, the Scotsman Percy Pilcher achieved success with his glider just before the start of this century, but he too died whilst pioneering the principles of flight. Already he had designed and partially built a powered aeroplane and, if he had lived, might have been the first to succeed.

Even before man-lifting gliders flew successfully, many people endeavoured to achieve powered flight with steam engines; early and serious attempts were made by L P Frost of Cambridge, who, from 1868 onwards, aimed to fly by following the wing-flapping principles of birds. His ornithopters were developed over about eight years and, to take the bird image to its limit, he copied the wing pattern of the crow, scaling up the precise shape and position of each feather; his principle, presumably, was that if it worked for the crow it should do so for man. This steam engine, an Ahrbecker of 5 hp (an original specimen of which is on show in the Collection) weighed 110 lb and failed to produce the energy needed to flap the wings with sufficient power and the project failed. In 1908, though, the Royal Aeronautical Society declared that if the power had been available the Frost ornithopter should have flown successfully.

The petrol engine saw daylight in 1885 on the first motor-carriage (a three-wheeler produced by Benz), followed a year later by Daimler with a four-stroke motor-cycle, but designers' efforts to harness this for the aeroplane were thwarted by heavy weight and low output. Although the Wrights established world fame by their success with their powered Flyer 1, their practical knowledge had been based on four years' experience, firstly with a towed kite in 1899 and afterwards by man-carrying gliders. In practice, the Wrights deserve credit for much more than their initial achievement in 1903, for a year later they were flying circuits; when Wilbur gave demonstrations in France in 1908 his proof of success and knowledge spurred the Europeans into action. Before then, on this side of the Atlantic, efforts had been only marginally successful and the Wrights were many years ahead. Although most people realize that the Wrights designed their own aircraft, not all appreciate that they designed their own engine and remarkably efficient propellers which rotated in opposite directions and were geared down to rotate at less than engine speed in order to obtain maximum performance. They built a working wind-tunnel in which to test their theories and a repro-duction of this exists at Old Warden.

In model form the Collection houses specimens of two very early flying machines. One is a large scale model of the original Wright Flyer 1, made especially to complete the Collection's range of exhibits from the birth of powered flight. The second item displays the ideas and constructional methods behind the British Matchless, a design patented in 1909 by Arthur Phillips of Market Drayton in Shropshire, who was a cycle maker. This is unusual because it was one of the earliest 'convertiplanes', in which the propellers could be rotated in pitch to provide power for either vertical or horizontal flight. A motor-cycle engine enabled the original machine to make several successful tethered flights, but development ceased before its intended power unit — a two-stroke air-cooled rotary engine of Mr Phillips' own design — was ready to use. The principle of vertical/horizontal power deflection has been studied at intervals throughout the progress of flight; today's Harrier is the logical outcome.

At this stage we turn our concentration towards the full-size aeroplane, the basic layout of which tended to stabilize over the few years before the First World War.

Right: The 1910 Deperdussin.

As birds are monoplanes, it is natural for many early designers to have followed suit. There were exceptions, of course, and those who saw the famous film *Those Magnificent Men in their Flying Machines* may well have a rather imaginative idea of the variety of ways in which man aimed to take to the air.

We claim that we live in an active, do-it-yourself era, but the efforts of the first aviation pioneers place us all in a rather dark shadow. In the very early nineteen hundreds, the unknown elements of flight were almost countless: the precise wing shape and areas needed to obtain the required lift; the thickness of materials needed for the structure, to avoid failure through weakness or through being too heavy to fly; the controls needed to achieve success in all three flight axes; how to transmit power from a heavy, low-energy engine through a propeller (which itself needed to be of practical design) rather than through road wheels; and if the machine should fly, how to manage it in the air.

Often these and the other associated problems were tackled by one man who designed, built and flew the end product. This gave early aviation a very important personal touch that remained in the industry until the numerous smaller firms were progressively incorporated into impersonalized units. Today, alas, even these have been swept into oblivion.

Let us take a broad look at the aeroplane up to 1912. As evidence of the monoplane trend which was particularly strong in Europe, the Collection contains three specimens from that period: two from France and one of British brew. All have their wing loads taken externally, with pylons above the fuselages from which wires are run to attachment points at roughly mid-span to take the landing stresses; from beneath, attached to the undercarriage structure, similar wires run upwards and are attached to the wing undersurfaces to take the flying loads. This arrangement formed the basis on which the braced monoplane became a practical proposition.

Rudders, already with many years of waterborne proving behind them, were an obvious requirement and were brought into use as hinged surfaces from the start; often they formed the sole vertical tail element, while some early designers introduced the fixed fin to provide additional directional stability. Logically, movable elevators mounted on fixed horizontal tailplanes were soon the accepted norm, although some machines had elevators only, with no fixed tailplanes; these perhaps, can bear some comparison with many of today's designs with their all-moving horizontal tail surfaces.

It was in lateral control that the pioneers used a method that is wholly foreign to the modern mind. Instead of having hinged ailerons, one of which would move up and the other down as the column was moved sideways, the wing structure itself was built with a flexibility that enabled the equivalent result to be achieved by twisting: this became known as wing-warping. With the wheel turned to the left, effectively the wing on that side would reduce both in incidence and in lift-generating shape towards the tip, while the right wing tip would increase in camber and angle and therefore provide additional lift, producing a rolling motion to the left. Although this method of roll control worked reasonably well, it proved to be imprecise and sometimes unpredictable, so the separate hinged aileron came into its own quite early in the development process.

Some features of the first aeroplanes disappeared from popularity to re-appear many years later. I have mentioned the control wheel, which on many pioneer machines was turned, in its logical sense, either to warp the wings or to move the ailerons, but for crispness of control this was soon succeeded by the single control column, or joystick, used on nearly all machines for many years; eventually the wheel returned to use, firstly on the heavier aircraft and gradually, in the form of the yoke, it crept back into the lighter types and today there are many more machines with half-wheels than with sticks. Also, the 1907 and 1909 Bleriots had tailwheels, but most later machines had skids at the rear; tail wheels (which were really practicable only when brakes were fitted) were not in full use again until well into the thirties.

The popular monoplane principle developed not only in performance and all-round capability, but noticeably in appearance. The Bleriot XI's rear fuselage structure was uncovered and fully exposed for all to see, while the Deperdussin, little over a year younger, was fully dressed. Both had their tiny engines mounted externally on the fronts of the fuselages, but by 1911 Robert Blackburn's Mercury monoplane had a neat cowling covering the top half of its rotary radial engine. The Bleriot and Blackburn machines make interesting comparisons on a feature-by-feature basis, on progress generally and especially on cleanness of design.

Not all designers favoured the monoplane; biplanes and triplanes played leading parts in the progressive development of the aeroplane and examples of both are displayed at Old Warden. The 1910 Bristol Boxkite (exhibited in reproduction form), developed from the famous Henry Farman, sported many unusual features, including a controllable foreplane, a biplane tail, three rudders, a four-wheel undercarriage, a pusher propeller, ailerons and a control stick. By contrast, A V Roe's Triplane of the same year, although again using four main-wheels, had the more customary warping wings and (apart from the third wing) a generally more conventional layout.

Boxkites and even Bleriots had limited roles in the military field, but most machines produced before 1912 were intended and used mainly to pioneer the principles and performance of controlled flight. Air races and long distance contests, with significant awards for the winners, encouraged those with the urge to fly — and those with the foresight to sell flying, in the form of aeroplanes or lessons, or both — to compete to make powered aircraft as practicable as possible. That they were developed more rapidly than anyone could have anticipated was brought-about largely by the outside influence of war, but still today, a human touch is added to the scene when we realize that all the subsequent development, to Concorde and space flight, has occurred in little more than the lifespan of an average person.

The Pressure of War

The first flying machines were just that; they had no roles to perform other than the essential achievement of successful flight. This is logical in the early evolution process, but clearly there would be many functions for which an aeroplane would be tasked. War was one. Although at the outbreak of the Great War in 1914 military aeronautical activity was both minimal and disorganized, with considerable opposition from the diehards who predicted that the aeroplane could be no match for the horse, very little time passed between the light and relatively flimsy pre-war structures and the strong, work-horse machines of the mid-teens. Perhaps the production Blackburn monoplane of 1912 and the appearance of the Bristol Fighter only four years later can bring home this point most effectively.

Just as the aeroplanes of the Air Battalion of the Royal Engineers (which merged in 1912 into the Royal Flying Corps) and the first equipment of the Royal Naval Air Service could not be described as machines with obvious fighting potential, the available equipment with which to wage war in the air was equally sparse. Although wireless communication was tried experimentally in the earliest days, suitable sets were not regularly available and other methods were used for passing information; message streamers, for example, were dropped for passing details of the enemy's whereabouts. On the fighting front, re-volvers or rifles were used from cockpits, and these led to very personal duels between individual opponents; some bombs, including the 20 lb Hale, existed from the outset and grenades were dropped, but even darts — or flechettes as they were called — were released from cockpits. For a short time these were dropped in large numbers onto troop concentrations in the hope that quantity would produce devastating results, but there is little evidence that they were particularly effective.

Specimens of these early tools of war are displayed in the Collection with uniforms, helmets, flight instruments (note the size of the airspeed indicator used in the Handley Page 0/400 of 1917) and documents relating to the whole 1914-18 era. But perhaps one of the most significant achievements of the mid-war period was the ability to fire a fixed forward-facing machine-gun through the arc of a revolving propeller. This was achieved by synchoniz-ing gears, well-known examples of which were the Constantinesco (hydraulic) and Sopwith-Kauper (mechan-ical) interruptor gears; these devices had a major impact on the ability of the aeroplane to engage in serious combat; the gun could be mounted on top of the fuselage, within reach of the pilot, who not only aimed it (and his aeroplane) at the target, but could deal with technical management of the gun itself. A diagram is on display to show the way in which the hydraulic interruptor gear worked.

The aeroplane and its equipment developed together; the flexible monoplane structure with its need for bracing from above and below gave way to a biplane layout that offered several advantages. Admittedly an extra wing generated more drag (wind resistance) but this was relatively uncritical at the low speeds of the time; more important was the biplane's additional lift, which helped in carrying the heavier loads associated with a military operation. However, the biplane's main advantage was its structural rigidity, for gone were the pylons, to be replaced by streamlined inter-plane struts near the tips and strong attachments or mountings to the fuselage at the inboard ends of the wings. The biplane, too, could have a smaller span for a given weight-lifting ability, and this improved both the roll rate and overall manoeuvrability.

There were a few exceptions to the biplane trend, but the 1914-18 aeroplanes on view at Old Warden are representative of the general concept of the time. A remarkable commonality existed; most machines were single-engine tractor (i.e. propeller at the front) biplanes, with two main-wheels and tailskids and, for those accom-modating two crew members, cockpits in tandem. Perhaps some of the greatest variations were in engine design; in the early part of the war, the rotary radial achieved both success and fame. On this, the crankshaft was fixed to the airframe structure and the crankcase and cylinders revolved around it. There was no carburettor as such; petrol was delivered through the hollow crankshaft and the air/fuel ratio was controlled by the pilot with two side-by-side levers to enable him to achieve the required fine adjustment; this was critical, too, for either a lean or a rich mixture would produce a power cut, so once the day's optimum setting (which varied with temperature, pressure, humidity and other factors) had been found by pre-take-off experiment, many pilots tended to leave this well alone. Then performance control was the work of the 'blip switch'; this was a button on the stick, which, when depressed, cut out the ignition, the power returning when the button was released.

Rotary engines had short working lives, many being cleared for only fifty hours between overhauls, but aeroplanes' operational lives, too, were usually clipped prematurely in battle or in accident, so this was not its most serious shortcoming. The disadvantage was that the large, heavy rotating mass produced strong gyroscopic effects, so that when turning in one direction the nose of the aircraft tended to fall and, in turning the other way, to rise. This made manoeuvring and accurate gun-sighting difficult and had restricting effects on the tactics of the time.

When running well, with all cylinders firing, the rotary was a remarkably smooth power source, and the reliability record was better than one might expect from an all-moving engine; but, although used in trainers for many more years, by 1917 its operational heyday had passed. The static engine had been developed to a remarkable performance level, with the Rolls-Royce Falcon producing 275 hp and heralding a design layout that held (and perhaps led) the field for thirty years. A liquid-cooled engine with twelve cylinders in a V layout, the Falcon's logical and progressively developed successors included the Kestrel, Merlin and Griffon, the last of which served until mid-1992 when the Royal Air Force retired the final few Shackletons. It is unlikely that any basic concept (except, perhaps, the wing!) has remained to the fore for such a large percentage of aviation's history to date.

Although the aeroplanes of the 1914-18 war live on at Old Warden, to be seen statically at close quarters on any day and occasionally in the air, we must not forget the people involved. The flying personnel, with descriptive showcases devoted to the achievements of such aces as Major James McCudden and Captain Albert Ball, VC (both of whom flew Royal Aircraft Factory S.E.5s that were similar to the example now on display) are key figures, but no aeroplane has been able to fly without the hard and skilled efforts of those whose work has remained unsung; not only the ground crews in the field, but also the hundreds of women who sewed the fabric that covered the greater part of all the aeroplanes of the time. Photographs of these, too, serve to remind us of the national effort behind the wartime aviation scene.

Many readers may be surprised at the scale of the flying operation in the first war. More than eight thousand Avro 504s were built and, although accident rates were high with frequent write-offs, in November 1918 the Royal Air Force had 22,647 aeroplanes on active strength. This is twice as many as the total number of aeroplanes on the UK register today! Only a few of these veterans have survived, but the representative types on show serve as rare reminders of one of the most hectic periods of aerial activity that the world has known.

Private Flying between the Wars

At the end of World War I hundreds of surplus military aeroplanes became available for civil use and these were sold at prices that were tiny fractions of their original costs. Many were handled by the Aircraft Disposal Company and among the types to find ready buyers were the Avro 504 and S.E.5a, each of which is on show at Old Warden. On a smaller scale, attempts were made by the manufacturers to convert machines on their existing production lines into civilian material; the Sopwith Aviation Company's two-seat Dove (as an on-the-line modification from the military single-seat Pup) was one example, but for reasons of expense most sales were centred on the surplus machines that had seen varying amounts of military service.

This ready supply of serviceable aeroplanes, some of which were nearly new, virtually eliminated any immediate post-war demand for new conventional light civil aeroplanes, so the makers turned their minds to economy in a manner that would be appropriate in today's approaching energy crisis. The aim was to obtain maximum performance from minimum power, resulting in quite fantastic returns of miles flown for each gallon used. In 1923 the English Electric Wren, with its diminutive two-cylinder ABC engine of only 398 cc, competed with success at the *Daily Mail* Light Aeroplane Contest at Lympne in Kent by covering 87.5 miles on one gallon.

In the same year Geoffrey de Havilland came forward with the little DH 53, a single-seater powered by a range of small engines including the 750 cc Douglas, 698 cc Blackburn Tomtit and the Bristol Cherub. Although it flew successfully, experience proved it to be too small for really practical use; the DH 51, by contrast, was a moderate-size biplane that could seat two or three people, but this, too, failed to fill a need in the market. Not to be beaten, the de Havilland name excelled itself when the first DH 60 Moth appeared. In effect this was a mid-way design between the extremes of the DH 51 and 53, but if ever a compromise could be successful, the Moth proved the point.

Perhaps the Moth is the most significant of the production light aeroplanes of the period shortly after World War I. With the supply of former military machines exhausted and with light aeroplane clubs being formed in many parts of Britain, by 1925 a new market had materialised. The Moth was ideal; simple, rugged, reliable and economical, yet large and powerful enough for serious flights to be carried out effectively, it filled the bill for training, touring, competitions and record-breaking.

Right: The Gladiator immediately after landing. Note the very small flaps beneath all four wings.

Private and sporting flying would have grown in popularity far less rapidly if the DH 60 had been missing from the inventory. From the original design, the Moth breed later extended into a range of machines to suit all tastes, contributing in no small way to Britain's reputation for producing the world's most successful light aircraft. Other manufacturers followed in attempts to fill the new demand, but none quite managed to equal the magic of the Moths.

The two-seat open biplane, in most cases with cockpits in tandem, was the norm of the day, but some designers spread their thoughts in many directions to produce machines ranging from single-seat ultra-lights, suitable for amateur construction, to refined cabin monoplanes for those seeking comfort, speed and range. The contrasting results can be seen at Old Warden today in the Flying Flea and the Percival Gull-Six. The first, of French origin, with a top speed of about 60 mph behind (among others) a Scott motorcycle engine of 16 hp, was intended to be suitable for the absolute beginner who could build it and then teach himself to fly it; the second offered 200 hp, a top speed of about 175 mph and a cabin for three. Both are described separately in the book, but by mentioning them together we can appreciate the diversity of ideas and needs that were spreading into the realm of the light aeroplane; similar extremes exist today although, alas, in recent years there have been no British machines to maintain the national reputation built up in the twenties and thirties. Certainly one type of training/touring/aerobatic monoplane — the Slingsby T-67 — is in production; however, it has entered the sales arena at a very difficult time to make a deep penetration into the civil market, although recent contracts for the United States Air Force and as a trainer on which Royal Air Force pilots will receive their initial tuition should ensure its future.

The Collection is fortunate to hold a very broad range of civil types of the period between the wars, when the use and development of the true light aeroplane reached its climax. One hangar, opened in 1982, houses an exclusive range of aircraft of de Havilland origin, while another covers the field of products of the other manufacturers of the time. No one should deny the practical value of the designs of the seventies and eighties, for some very usable aircraft are available on the world market, but values have changed. Today the main aims are to produce aircraft that are geared to quantity production, easy to fly and which can accommodate advanced avionics (radio equipment) to simplify the task of navigating en route and letting down to aerodromes in bad weather. From a workaday angle, these intentions are wholly logical and beneficial, but by eliminating the need for accurate handling and reducing the requirement for such a built-in consciousness of wind and weather, the modern designer has deprived pilots of many of the skills and pleasures that

have been associated with pure flying for its own sake.

A modern aeroplane with a nosewheel undercarriage is easy to steer on the ground and the tendency to weathercock into wind is noticeable only in the roughest conditions, while the light aeroplane pilot in a biplane with a brakeless tail-skid undercarriage needs to work constantly with throttle, rudder and sometimes aileron to attain and maintain the desired headings. An out-of-wind take-off in the earlier machine calls for comparable skills; once in the air balanced flight requires co-ordinated use of hands and feet with accurate use of the rudder to match the control in roll; even more, a landing on all three points results only from a well-adjusted approach at the right speed, with accurate judgment of the height and rate of hold-off; keeping straight at the end of a landing run in certain conditions can demand rapid response with rudder before a slight swing develops into something worse.

More about flying a typical biplane of the period between the wars appears in a later chapter and detailed handling descriptions of many of the historic aeroplanes are contained in a companion volume to this book (*From Bleriot to Spitfire: flying the historic aeroplanes of the Shuttleworth Collection*), but the marked changes in flight characteristics that have occurred in the recent post-war years have made the modern light aeroplane into something that is so fundamentally different from its predecessor of fifty or so years ago. That in itself enhances the value of the range of earlier types housed in the Collection and adds to the importance of keeping these machines in flying condition.

Leading into World War II

The development of military aircraft has been a start-and-stop operation throughout the history of Service aviation. This has been dictated almost entirely by the degree of urgency for an effective fighting force and the directly-related funds that were available. After rapid progress throughout the 1914-18 war, culminating in such effective operational types as the Bristol Fighter, S.E.5a and, ultimately, the Sopwith Snipe, the military flying-machine made virtually no progress for about a decade. Numbers of aircraft, too, fell dramatically, from a total of 22,647 on RAF strength (with 188 operational squadrons) at the time of the Armistice to a mere twelve first-line squadrons by the end of 1919.

Although the following years saw a slow growth again in numerical strength, there was little sign of really new equipment. One squadron of Snipes served as Great Britain's only fighter defence until late in 1922 and, despite its outdated rotary engine, the type remained on first-line strength until eight years after the war. The ubiquitous

Bristol Fighter saw extended service on numerous duties, especially army co-operation, for fourteen years of post-armistice peace, while the trainer version served with the Oxford and Cambridge University Air Squadrons into the thirties. The Avro 504, too, enjoyed a long life; its post-war development, from the rotary-engined K variant to the 504N with an Armstrong-Siddeley Lynx static radial, proved the value of the original design as well as indicating the financially frugal atmosphere prevailing at the time. In 1931 504Ns pioneered the art of serious tuition in instrument flying and remained in use at flying training schools until finally replaced in 1933, mainly by the Avro Tutor from the same stable.

Because of the long service provided by these 1914-18 designs, readers will not be surprised to find a gap of ten years between the end of hostilities and the date of the first true post-war military type to be represented in the Collection. Even this was a trainer, in the form of the little Hawker Tomtit that was one of two machines to compete for the task of replacing the Avro 504N. Also, visitors to Old Warden are able to see the larger Avro Tutor, which was the Tomtit's rival that eventually won the main production contract for the RAF. More surprising to many, though, will be the fact that the de Havilland Tiger Moth, known mainly as an elementary trainer used in large numbers during World War II, entered service before the Tutor and served briefly at No.3 Flying Training School during 1932

before the Tutor replaced it. Several years later this process was reversed!

Throughout the period of peace in the twenties and most of the thirties, relatively few real changes emerged either in the basic design layouts of the aircraft in use or in the roles that they performed. On the operational side, perhaps the long line of Hawker biplanes that served so well as fighters, light bombers, army co-operation and general duties machines typified the commonality of the military flying scene of the time. All were strut-braced biplanes, with fixed undercarriages, open cockpits, and all, except the single-seat Fury, accommodated two in tandem; they had fixed-pitch propellers and other basic features that had applied to most types designed and produced during the earlier war. In most cases bombs were hung externally, radio of any sort was an exception rather than the rule and armament remained thin; even the Fury fighter had only two guns whilst the Hind general-purpose light bomber of late 1935 retained the World War I practice of one fixed forward-firing Vickers and one movable Lewis machine-gun. The main progress in nearly twenty years related to steady increases in power, with the Rolls-Royce Kestrels of both the Fury and Hind

XV Squadron past and present: the Collection's Hind in the foreground, with a Tornado behind.

producing 640 hp compared with the 275 hp of the Rolls-Royce Falcon in the 1917 Bristol Fighter. The latter and the Hind make interesting comparisons; both can be studied on a tour of the Old Warden hangars.

By the mid-thirties more positive signs of progress started to emerge. The Gloster Gladiator single-seat fighter serves as a prime preserved example to show the change from the traditional to the new; although a biplane with a fixed undercarriage, the production Gladiator (which entered service in February 1937 with No. 72 Squadron) had an effective armament of four fixed guns, an enclosed cockpit with a sliding canopy and wing flaps. In some ways it boasted many of the features of the future that were to be found on the Hurricanes and Spitfires which followed the Gladiator into service, to make it the RAF's last-ever biplane fighter.

The change from the strut-braced biplane to the cantilever monoplane, on which all the structural strength was contained within the airframe, with need for neither struts nor bracing wires, called for a trainer of similar layout. So from Air Ministry specification T.40/36 came the Miles Magister, an open cockpit tandem two-seat low-wing monoplane with split flaps, a tailwheel, brakes, blind-flying hood and clearance for all normal aerobatic manoeuvres. Ironically, this machine that was so modern in appearance moved backwards in one sense, for gradually, beneath the visible surface, the long line of traditional biplanes produced between the wars had changed in construction materials and methods from all-wood to mainly metal structures. The Magister was all wood, as was its bigger and more powerful brother, the Master advanced trainer.

In a comparatively short time the biplane almost disappeared from the Service scene, but there were a few exceptions; the Tiger Moth continued in use as an elementary trainer until after World War II, the Dominie twin-engine radio trainer and communications machine (a military variant of the Dragon-Rapide short-haul airliner) lasted almost as long and the Swordfish naval torpedo-carrier seemed to go on for ever.

The big change, however, had come to stay — and had come with a rush. Monoplane bombers such as the Fairey Battle, Bristol Blenheim, Handley Page Hampden and Vickers Wellington, and their fighter counterparts in the Hawker Hurricane and Supermarine Spitfire, entered squadron service within a few months of each other in 1937 and 1938. Alas, many of these types that saw active service in the early part of the war, together with later designs, such as the Short Stirling heavy bomber, have not survived into the present era of aircraft preservation. In the main, and understandably, the larger the type the less is the likelihood that it would be saved from the scrap-man's axe; but the Hurricane and the Spitfire remain with us today and specimens have been preserved by

the Shuttleworth Collection. The Hurricane — an early Canadian-built Mark I that operated from a merchant ship in 1941 — is the oldest complete specimen of the type. The Spitfire saw operational service with a Czech squadron.

As the Shuttleworth Collection aims to show the earlier days of the development of the flying machine, World War II has been selected as a broad cut-off point. Many other collections contain aircraft of the post 1939-45 period, so the Trustees consider that to duplicate these efforts would weaken the limited resources at Old Warden that are available for tending the needs of the true veterans. However, as there is no other preserved range of elementary/basic trainers that have been used by the flying Services since military aviation began in 1910, Old Warden's hangars house one post-war type, the 1950 de Havilland Chipmunk.

The Chipmunk has two special claims to fame, for despite the much-acclaimed records of long service for both the Avro 504 series and the Tiger Moth, it has beaten both by very considerable margins and in 1980 re-entered regular RAF use as a primary trainer. Also, it is the last in the line of de Havilland light aeroplanes. The Chipmunks now operating are almost forty-five years of age and, although the numbers in service are being reduced, some may remain active until the start of the 21st century.

The end of World War II saw the most dramatic change in the characteristics of military aircraft. Although the Gloster Meteor jet fighter saw limited operational service in 1945, the other types in service were piston-engined, nearly all with traditional tailwheel undercarriages and other features that were soon to be lost for ever. Handling and operating techniques changed, with the newer types generally easier to fly (no swing on take-off with a jet, whereas this was a major feature on powerful piston-powered machines) but more tricky to operate, mainly because of very high fuel consumption at low levels.

So there are several reasons supporting the Shuttleworth Collection's policy to use the 1939-45 war as the end of an era in the history of the military flying-machine. The aircraft to be seen at Old Warden form a unique range and most of the aeroplanes on display are the World's sole surviving flying examples of their types. This adds to the significance of the exhibition; also it increases the value of a long and detailed study of the aircraft that are described in the pages that follow.

3
The Historic Aeroplanes
in Chronological Order

1909: BLERIOT TYPE XI   Acquired 1935

Span: 29 ft
Empty weight: 484 lb
Power: 24 hp Anzani 3-cylinder fan

Louis Bleriot just managed to get into the air in 1907, in his tandem-wing machine *Libellule*. In the same year he produced his more conventional Bleriot No. VII which was the first-ever monoplane with a tractor engine, enclosed fuselage, rear mounted tail unit, and two-wheel main undercarriage, with a tail-wheel; shortly after came his No. VIII which, surprisingly, had ailerons. The Bleriot XI, however, reverted to wing-warping for lateral control and it was the first of his designs to be wholly successful; in this he proved the possibility of cross-country flying on 13 July 1909 by covering twenty-five miles from Etampes to Orleans at a maximum height of about seventy-five feet. This achievement opened his mind to the practicability of a Channel crossing, which had been unsuccessfully attempted by an Antoinette monoplane only six days after Bleriot's first cross-country.

Soon after 0430 on Sunday 25 July 1909, Louis Bleriot took off from the French coast and forty minutes later he crash-landed in a field near Dover Castle, to become the first person to cross the English Channel in an aeroplane. The early start was necessary for several reasons: calm conditions were needed to ensure full controllability of the machine and a low temperature was required to provide a cool charge for the small engine. The Anzani produced barely enough power for long sustained flight and many say that a brief rain shower cooled it sufficiently to help to keep it running, although a recent check on several contemporary daily newspapers reveals no trace of this. If the shower story is true, is it possible that, unwittingly, Bleriot was a pioneer in gaining benefits from water injection?

Following this success, Bleriot's monoplanes sold well and many flying schools adopted them as standard trainers. They were used in races and competitions and even in military roles. A Bleriot with the more powerful 50 hp Gnome rotary engine was used for the first aerial post from Hendon to Windsor in September 1911.

The Exhibit: BAPC 3. Basically similar to the machine used for the Channel crossing, this machine (constructor's No. 14) was one of the original aircraft on the Bleriot School at Hendon in 1910. It crashed in 1912, was stored under Blackfriars railway bridge and acquired by A E Grimmer who rebuilt and flew it. Richard Shuttleworth obtained it in 1935 as his first historic aeroplane and flew it in RAeS garden parties in 1937, '38 and '39. Today, it is restricted to straight hops across the aerodrome, but possibly is the world's oldest aeroplane with the earliest aero-engine in flying condition.

1910: DEPERDUSSIN

Acquired 1935

Span: 28 ft 9 ins
Empty weight: 500 lb
Power: 35 hp Anzani Y-type

During the short period between the birth of the Bleriot XI and ·the dimensionally similar Deperdussin, the Anzani engine had been developed from an out-of-balance fan layout to a more practicable Y shape that led to the later introduction of the popular and successful radial. The smoother running that this produced, together with a thirty per cent increase in output, the sleeker design of the aeroplane and a totally covered fuselage, combined to produce a performance, which though hardly startling, made sustained flight a more regular reality.

The makers produced these machines in quantity to equip flying schools in Britain and on the Continent, with a selling price for the 'Popular' model set at £460. Although the Bleriot's earlier Channel crossing had made international history, the Deperdussin proved its practicability not by virtual wave or hedge-hopping, but by sustained cross-country flights at safer altitudes; in 1911 one came third in the *Daily Mail* Circuit of Britain contest, flying from Hendon to Edinburgh, across to Glasgow and then via Carlisle, Manchester, Bristol, Exeter, Salisbury and Brighton to the famous historic flying ground at Brooklands.

Throughout the history of aviation, successful airframe designs have been developed by fitting more powerful engines. The 'Dep' was no exception and, as with the Bleriot, the 50 hp Gnome rotary was a logical and successful choice. Later, two and three-seater versions were produced, each using Gnomes of higher power. In various forms and with engines of up to 100 hp, Deperdussins achieved many successful flights and established a share of records. A developed racing version achieved 124 mph in 1913, compared with the maximum of 55 mph credited to the basic machine; a seaplane version with a Gnome developing 160 hp won the first Schneider Trophy race at Monaco, achieving 127 mph. The pilot was Maurice Prevost.

The Exhibit: BAPC 4. A school or 'Popular' version, it is believed to be the 43rd to have been built, in 1910, and used at Hendon until offered for sale in damaged form in 1914. As with the Collection's Bleriot, it became the property of A E Grimmer, who repaired and flew it from the polo ground near Bedford. When acquired by Richard Shuttleworth in 1935, it was in poor condition and it was renovated at Old Warden to fly again in 1937. Stored throughout World War II, it has flown several times in recent years and when weather conditions are ideal it is capable of completing a half circuit of the aerodrome, although normally it is restricted to 'straights'.

1910: BRISTOL BOXKITE   Acquired 1966

Span: 34 ft 6 ins (upper mainplanes; military version
   46 ft 6 in)
Empty weight: 800 lb (military 900 lb)
Engines: Various, including 50 hp and 70 hp Gnome rotary
   (This specimen has a modern 90 hp Lycoming)

In 1907 Henry Farman, often referred to as Henri Farman, but who was an Englishman living in France, started to modify a Voisin biplane to improve its performance and handling qualities. By 1909 he had designed his own machine, which he called Henry Farman III, and this proved to be one of the greatest aeroplanes of its time. Many people copied it and, in Britain, the result was the Bristol Boxkite.

The Boxkite was a striking sight; with elevators ahead of and behind the mainplanes, a biplane tail, three rudders and a pusher propeller, its prospects were based on refining and improving the Farman design, starting life with the bonus of a successful and well-proven type record behind it. Although essentially civil in origin, the Boxkite had clear military potential; in March 1911 four examples were ordered by the War Office at a time when many senior officers and politicians were opposed to the introduction of the aeroplane which, they insisted, could never replace the horse. A developed Service variant sported an additional twelve feet of span to the upper wing, to enable it to carry heavier loads.

Unlike many machines of the period, the Boxkite used ailerons for lateral control; but they were different from later ailerons, for they had no balance cables and hung 'limp' until the machine moved and the airflow lifted them into the flying attitude.

Boxkites were used in many parts of the world, including Australia and India; they were the first British aircraft to be ordered for export, with eight for the Imperial Russian Army. Although very successful, the type was cumbersome and had a relatively short life, with the last specimen flying in Australia late in 1915.

The Exhibit: BAPC 2. One of only four aircraft in the Collection that is not a genuine original historic machine, the Boxkite is a reproduction built by F G Miles Ltd at Shoreham for the film *Those Magnificent Men in their Flying Machines*. As no original Boxkite exists, the Bristol Aeroplane Co Ltd acquired this specimen when the filming was finished and passed it to the Collection for preservation. In the air it is a most impressive sight, but it is flown only in conditions of almost complete calm.

It has very difficult handling characteristics, but in 1989 the weight of the tail unit was reduced and subsequently the angle of incidence of the tailplane was lowered. First flight after the later modification was on 10 April 1992; the handling and performance have improved significantly.

1910: AVRO TRIPLANE IV   Acquired 1966

Span: 32 ft (bottom wing 20 ft)
Empty weight: 650 lb
Power: 35 hp Green in-line (water-cooled)
(This specimen has a 105 hp Cirrus Hermes II of 1927)

A V Roe, who was one of Britain's most famous early
pioneers, broke away from the usual monoplane or
biplane layout and decided that a third set of wings would
provide the lifting performance that he sought. He
designed and built four such machines, which flew
successfully, but which were used only for test and
development. No version of the Avro Triplane was put into
quantity production, but experience with these machines
enabled him to design a highly successful biplane in the
Avro 504; this, from 1913 onwards and in a variety of
versions, became the first really effective dual-control
training aeroplane to be used on a large scale and the
type remained in use into the thirties.

The triplane layout was based largely on a search for
wings with a long span relative to the width (chord),
resulting in what is known technically as a high aspect
ratio. This has certain aerodynamic advantages, stemming
from the early discovery that most lift comes from the front
portion, or just behind the leading edge of a wing, so the
greater the span, the greater the lift that is produced.
Another important advantage, however, is that the higher
this ratio, the less the induced drag that is generated,
therefore producing a better performance for a given
power output. The Triplane IV had a remarkable aspect
(span-to-chord) ratio of more than nine-to-one; clearly it
proved its worth, for both the Avro 504 and the later Avro
Tutor had wings that were long in relation to their width.

The Triplane had a control wheel, which, when turned,
twisted the shape of the outer sections of the two upper
sets of wings, to provide lateral control through wing
warping. The shorter bottom wing, mounted below and
clear of the fuselage so that lift could be generated
throughout its span, was not connected to the control
system.

The name Avro, derived from A V Roe, lived in the lead
of famous British aeroplanes through both world wars and
beyond; the Anson and the Lancaster are household
names, while the Vulcan, which remained in service with
the Royal Air Force into the mid-eighties, also is of Avro
origin.

The Exhibit: BAPC 1. With the Boxkite this shares the
claim to be a relatively recently-built machine, for this too,
was constructed for the film *Those Magnificent Men in
their Flying Machines*, by the Hampshire Aeroplane Club
at Eastleigh, Southampton. Although the original Roe
Triplane is in the Science Museum, this reproduction was
of considerable technical interest and an impressive flyer,
so the Trustees decided that it should be acquired to add
to the Collection.

1912: BLACKBURN

Acquired 1938

Span: 32 ft 1 in
Empty weight: 550 lb
Power: 50 hp Gnome rotary

Robert Blackburn was one of Britain's pioneers in designing and building aeroplanes. The first of his machines to fly successfully did so from the sands at Filey in 1910 and several developments followed over the next two years. The basic type became known as the Mercury and the machine in the Collection is the seventh and one of the last of that line, completed in 1912. By this time the design had improved into one of clean overall layout, with all surfaces fully covered and even a cowling round the top half of the engine, but still using wing-warping for lateral control.

The name of Blackburn survived until well after World War II when it became absorbed into Hawker-Siddeley Aviation. The Baffin, Shark, Skua, Roc and Botha are among the types remembered from that era, while among the last to emerge with the Blackburn prefix were the huge Beverley heavy transports for the RAF and the Buccaneer low-level strike aircraft. In addition to aeroplanes, the company produced numerous aero-engines including the Cirrus Major, the Cirrus Minor and the Bombardier. Also, the firm ran two reserve flying schools for the Royal Air Force and these were the only units to be equipped with the Blackburn B2 side-by-side biplane trainer; a flying specimen of this 1932 product is retained today at its birthplace of Brough in East Yorkshire.

The Exhibit: BAPC 5. This was built to the order of Cyril Foggin who learned to fly on a Bleriot at Eastbourne; later it was acquired by Francis Glew, but stored in 1914 and not discovered until 1937, largely hidden in a haystack. Then it was obtained by Richard Shuttleworth, who started to restore it, but work was not completed until 1949. In 1985 the Blackburn was wholly re-covered and the opportunity was taken to carry out some rectification including structural work. In calm conditions it flies a slow, majestic circuit and makes its mark as *the oldest genuine original British aeroplane still to fly anywhere in the world.*

1915: AVRO 504K

Acquired 1958

Span: 36 ft
Empty weight: 1231 lb
Power: 110 hp le Rhône rotary (but several others used)

Following A V Roe's experiments with a triplane formula, he continued his policy of using wings with high aspect ratio, but in biplane form. The result emerged as the Avro 504, which from its 1913 debut had an unusually long and successful career, at least four specimens surviving for impressment into military Service at the start of World War II.

The 504 entered the Royal Flying Corps as a fighting aeroplane and although used largely for observation purposes, bringing back information on enemy troop movements (against a strong resentment from the army commanders who saw no use for aircraft), the type was one of the first to be adapted for the bombing role; in November 1914 four Avro 504s made history by carrying out the first pre-planned bombing attack, with the Zeppelin works at Friedrichshafen as their target. It was in the training field, though, that the Avro 504 made its mark. Powered by the 100 hp Gnome Monosoupape, the 504J was the standard equipment of the School of Special Flying at Gosport in Hampshire where the Commanding Officer, Major R Smith-Barry, evolved the first organized pilot training system that formed the foundations of the RAF's later syllabus. Also it was the type on which King George VI learnt to fly. The K version, usually powered by the 100 hp le Rhône, but capable of taking a variety of rotary engines including the 130 hp Clerget and even the 150 hp Bentley BR-1, remained in RAF service until replaced in the late twenties by the Lynx-engined 504N.

Many surplus Ks were used after World War I by civil operators, mainly to provide joy-rides; individual modifications extended some of these into three or even four-seaters.

The Exhibit: H 5199. Built in 1918 as a K, converted in RAF service to a 504N and later civilianized as G-ADEV. Winner of the Devon Air Race in 1937 at 103 mph. Impressed into military service in 1940 as BK892 for glider towing experiments. Subsequently re-converted to original K standard by Avro apprentices for the Collection.

Suffered an engine failure in June 1989 when it landed among beetroot. Lack of spares delayed repair; flew again in July 1990, but still there were technical problems. More recently a different (but still original) engine has been fitted; adjustments and magneto changes have made the engine handling satisfactory.

1916: SOPWITH PUP   Acquired 1937

Span: 26 ft 6 in
Empty weight: 787 lb
Power: 80 hp le Rhône rotary

The Sopwith Pup was ordered early in 1916 for the Royal Naval Air Service and the type was used for trials of landing on the deck of a ship under way at sea, the results of which led to the development of the operational aircraft carrier. Later forming the equipment of several squadrons of the Royal Flying Corps, the Pup served with distinction on the Western Front from December 1916 onwards.

Although relatively low-powered, the Pup was manoeuvrable. Its light weight helped to provide a good rate of climb and an ability to hold its height in combat; successful encounters at 15,000 feet or more were not unknown. Standard armament was a single Vickers gun mounted in front of the pilot on top of the fuselage, synchronized to fire through the arc of the propeller by Sopwith-Kauper mechanical interrupter gear.

The operational life of the Pup was quite short by comparison with that of its higher-powered stablemate the Camel, but even the latter remained in squadron service for only a short time after the end of the war, when the Snipe replaced it. The Sopwith Aviation Company, though, endeavoured to put the last Pups on the production line into civilian use by converting them to two-seaters and using the appropriate peacetime name, Dove. Several modern reproductions of the Pup have been built.

The Exhibit: Constructor's No. W/O 3004/14. The last of ten Pups converted on the 1918 production line to two-seat civil Doves. Registered G-EBKY. Owned by C H Low-Wylde and based at West Malling; acquired by Richard Shuttleworth in 1936 and re-converted at Old Warden to original Pup standard. Not originally allocated a Service serial, so spuriously marked N5180, which was the Pup prototype.

On 4 August 1991, during a display at Old Warden, the engine cowling became detached and a textbook, if tearful, forced landing was made in an onion field. Interestingly, the logbook shows that a similar problem had occurred in 1920! Following rectification, the Pup flew again on 10 April 1992. Now carries serial N6181 with the word HAPPY on the fuselage sides and painted to represent Lt Cdr Breadner's machine of No 3 Naval Sqn.

1916: SOPWITH TRIPLANE

Built for the
Shuttleworth
Collection

Span: 26 ft 6 in
Empty weight: 1101 lb
Power: 130 hp Clerget rotary

The Sopwith Triplane served extensively with the Royal Naval Air Service and achieved considerable success as a fighting aeroplane. After Service trials in 1916, the Triplane played a leading part towards enabling Britain to achieve command of the air over the Western Front in the heavy fighting that occurred in 1917. Allegedly, the six Triplanes of B Flight of No. 10 Squadron, RNAS, alone destroyed no fewer than eighty-seven German aircraft between May and July 1917.

Despite the Triplane's achievements, the type's operational life was short, for by November 1917 the Sopwith Camel had replaced it in squadron use. It is a very appropriate machine for the Shuttleworth fleet, as fifty were built in Lincoln by Clayton and Shuttleworth before the firm's production was turned over to Camels.

The Exhibit: A reproduction aircraft, built over several years by members of Northern Aeroplane Workshops on an entirely voluntary basis. This specimen is so accurate in every way that during construction it received the approval of Sir Thomas Sopwith, who claimed that it could be considered as a one-off extension of his 1916 production line! Unfortunately Sir Thomas died in January 1989 — at the age of 101 — and was unable to see this machine in the air. It is powered by an original 130 hp Clerget rotary engine.

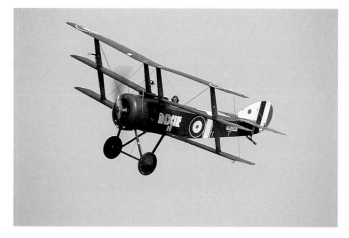

Although delivered to Old Warden at end of June 1990, low engine power output and misfiring caused delay to its completion; engine removed for checking and rectification of poor sealing of exhaust valve sets, distorted crankcase ('new' one drawn from stores), tight piston ring clearances, high oil flow and incompatible plugs. The engine was also statically balanced by selective assembly of components. Engine runs proved far more satisfactory, with the oil flow being reduced still further, and frequent changing of the exhaust valve springs, a weakness of the design of a Clerget. The first flight was on 10 April 1992 and after many tests the first-ever display appearance was on 27 June.

1917: BRISTOL F.2b   Acquired 1952

Span: 39 ft 3 in
Empty weight: 1934 lb
Power: 275 hp Rolls-Royce Falcon III V-12

The British and Colonial Aeroplane Company designed a number of aeroplanes after the Boxkite of 1910, so by 1916 considerable experience was available for the development of the Bristol Fighter. The type entered service with the Royal Flying Corps on the Western Front in March 1917. A large, rugged two-seater, the Bristol F.2b became well-respected by its opponents and earned the reputation of being the most effective fighting aeroplane of the First World War.

Various engines were used including the Hispano-Suiza, Siddeley Puma, Wolseley Viper and Sunbeam Arab, but the most successful was the Rolls-Royce Falcon liquid-cooled, twelve-cylinder Vee. Standard armament was a fixed Vickers gun firing forwards through the propeller arc with a Constantinesco synchronizing gear and one (sometimes two) Lewis gun(s) mounted on a Scarff ring and controlled by the rearward-facing observer. After initial difficulties, this back-to-back team-work proved very effective.

Although deservedly famous for its wartime success, the F.2b continued in production until 1926 and earned its reputation over a long period in service. Peacetime duties at home were largely on army co-operation work, while squadrons served overseas in such diverse areas as Germany, Turkey, Persia and India. The final role was as a dual-control trainer with Oxford and Cambridge University Air Squadrons, from which the type was retired in 1932.

The Exhibit: D 8096. Built in 1918. No wartime operational service, but with No. 208 Squadron in Turkey in 1923. Acquired in 1936 by Captain C P B Ogilvie, who stored it at Primrose Garages, Watford, with the aim of refurbishing to flying condition. Civil registration G-AEPH allotted but not used. Restored by the Bristol Aeroplane Company and first flown in Shuttleworth ownership in February 1952. After twenty-eight years with the Collection, underwent extensive engine and airframe refurbishing in Old Warden workshops in 1980-82.

Late in 1992 the engine (the oldest working Rolls-Royce aero-engine in the world) was replaced by an overhauled unit that had been on static display in the Collection. The engine that has been removed will be overhauled whilst the knowledge is still available and will be retained as a spare. First flew with 'new' engine on 10 March 1993. This aircraft has gained from sponsorship by Rolls-Royce plc.

1917: ROYAL AIRCRAFT FACTORY S.E.5a

Acquired 1957

Span: 26 ft 9 in
Empty weight: 1530 lb
Power: 200 hp Wolseley Viper V-8

The Royal Aircraft Factory at Farnborough (predecessor of the Royal Aerospace Establishment) designed and built the S.E.5 single-seat scout around the availability of the French 150 hp Hispano-Suiza engine. The type went into active service in France in April 1917. Modifications to the airframe and development of the geared engine to produce 200 hp resulted in the S.E.5a, which became one of the most successful fighters of the war. An alternative power source was the 200 hp Wolseley Viper, which was less complicated as it was a direct-drive engine.

Armed with two forward-firing machine-guns, with a Vickers on top of the fuselage (using synchronizing gear to avoid bullets hitting the propeller) and a Lewis mounted on top of the wing centre section and operated by a Bowden cable running to the cockpit, the S.E.5 and S.E.5a were the mounts of many of the aces of the time; among these were Major J McCudden and Captain Albert Ball, VC.

At the end of the war, sixteen squadrons of the Royal Air Force were equipped with the S.E.5a, but although its subsequent front-line military career lasted only a year or so, the type started a fresh civilian life; it proved popular as a sporting machine and competed in many air races (including the once-only Oxford and Cambridge Air Race of 1921 in which six participated), but its most notable peacetime achievement was in sky-writing. Major J C Savage's machines were in great demand for aerial advertising throughout Britain, while eleven S.E.5a's were used in the United States of America for similar work. The last airworthy S.E.5a in Britain made its final flight in 1937.

The Exhibit: Used in 1924 by Major Savage as G-EBIA. Found in 1955 hanging from the roof of the Armstrong-Whitworth flight shed at Whitley, near Coventry, and subsequently restored for the Collection by staff and apprentices at RAE Farnborough, where it first flew again in August 1959. Following problems with the Hispano-Suiza, the engine was changed in 1975 to a Wolseley Viper. Now flying in military markings with Service serial F904.

Following a final flight in September 1987 and discovery of metal in the filters, the Viper engine was removed for an extensive rebuild at RAE Bedford (Thurleigh). Flew again in April 1991. Although the airframe had always been Shuttleworth property, the engine was owned by RAE (later the Defence Research Agency) which handed over its interests on 21 October 1992.

Above: Twenty years of fighter development: the 1917 S.E.5a
leads the 1935 Gloster Gladiator before the latter was painted in
1990 in Battle of Britain markings.

1917: LUFT-VERKEHRS-GESELLSCHAFT LVG CVI

Acquired 1966

Span: 42 ft 5 in (upper wings)
Empty weight: 2090 lb
Power: 230 hp Benz upright in-line

The LVG CIV was the first aeroplane to make a daylight raid on London — in November 1916. A development, the CV, entered large scale service with the Imperial German Air Force and was used for observation and light bombing duties. The ultimate variant, the CVI, differed in having a deepened fuselage, reduced wing gap and a raised position for the observer-gunner to improve his field of view. Armament was a single fixed Spandau gun offset to the starboard side of the cockpit, firing forwards through the propeller and one movable Parabellum gun operated from the rear cockpit.

The LVG CVI was a strong and steady observation platform, but was large, heavy and relatively cumbersome on the handling side. Although it achieved considerable success in its intended role, lack of manoeuvrability made it a favourite target for British fighter pilots.

The Benz engine was a rugged, slow-revving unit with six cylinders in-line and a vertical exhaust stack giving the impression of a steam engine. This layout, while strange to British eyes, was used by the Germans on several other types.

Several CVIs were taken over at the end of the war and the type was extensively flight-tested for evaluation purposes in comparison with British types such as the Bristol Fighter.

The Exhibit: 7198/18 (the last figure indicating the year of manufacture). Believed to have been assembled from two or three machines captured in 1918; subsequently flown by the RAF at Martlesham Heath. Stored for many years by the Air Ministry Air Historical Branch and loaned for a time to the Science Museum, but not exhibited; appeared in mock combat with a Sopwith Triplane, a Bristol Fighter and S.E.5a at the 1937 Hendon Air Pageant. Passed to the Collection on long loan in 1966 and restored to flying condition at Old Warden, jointly by the Collection's engineering staff and specialist members of the Shuttleworth Veteran Aeroplane Society.

The engine has always tended to overheat due to the incorrect type of radiator (Renault car) fitted by the RAF in the 1950s. The cooling area is only about ⅔ of that required, but funds are not yet available for the correct type to be made and fitted.

1917: SOPWITH CAMEL

Loaned by
AJD Engineering 1992

Span: 28 ft
Empty weight: 1054 lb
Power: 110 hp le Rhône

The Sopwith Camel has been described as the most effective fighting British scout of the 1914-18 war. Following both the Pup and the Triplane into service, Camels first went into action with both the Royal Naval Air Service and the Royal Flying Corps in July 1917. Two reasons for the type's operational success were its extreme manoeuvrability and the fire power of its fixed twin Vickers guns. A later special Naval version had a fuselage with a detachable rear half to save space on ships.

Camels attained many successes, but perhaps the most renowned achievement was on 21 April 1918 when Captain R Brown shot down the famous (Captain) Baron Manfred von Richtofen from B7270, which was one of the machines built by Clayton and Shuttleworth. Regularly, Naval Camels intercepted Zeppelins over the North Sea, often operating from lighters fitted with small flight decks.

At the end of the war, Camels equipped 32 squadrons, all of which were part of the newly-formed Royal Air Force, although several of these had served previously with units of the Royal Naval Air Service. Despite its outstanding wartime success, the Camel's subsequent life in squadron service was short, for the rotary engine quickly became obsolete as more powerful static engines were developed.

The Exhibit: B6219 (G-ASOP). Built in September 1917, first with No 10 (Naval) Squadron and then serving until 1918 with the School of Aerial Warfare at Manston in Kent. Believed to have been bought post-war by 2 RFC pilots for commercial work in Lincoln area, but subsequently stored and rediscovered in 1963 by K C St Cyrien. Most restoration work carried out by British Aerospace at Kingston and later by British Caledonian at Gatwick. Acquired and stored by AJD Engineering at Ipswich for nearly 3 years and brought to Old Warden in April 1992. First flight at Old Warden on 27 July 1993.

1919: SOPWITH DOVE   Loaned 1992

Span: 24 ft 9½ in
Empty weight: 1065 lb
Power: 80 hp le Rhône rotary

The Dove was an early post-war attempt at a peaceful two-seat civil derivative of the Sopwith Pup single-seat scout. Apart from the second seat, the only significant structural alteration was sweepback on the mainplanes in order to accommodate the more backward position of the centre of gravity. The slight reduction in the span compared with the Pup is because of that revised wing layout.

Only ten Doves emerged from the Sopwith factory, all but one of which were two-seaters. One retained the single-seat layout of the Pup. Perhaps the most significant event in the type's career was a flight at Hounslow on 10 May 1919 in Dove G-EACM, in which the then Prince of Wales flew with Major W G Barker VC as pilot. This was

carried out at considerable displeasure of the Prince's father – King George V. Another, G-EAKH (re-registered in Australia as G-AUKH) was displayed at Melbourne Motor Exhibition in 1922. This was one of three sold to Australia. Despite the small production run, Doves were sold also to Canada, Sweden and Tasmania. The Collection's Pup was built as a Dove (G-EBKY) and was converted to a Pup in 1936-7 by Richard Shuttleworth.

The Exhibit: A replica built by Skysport Engineering. Allocated registration G-EAGA, allotted originally to a Dove sold abroad in September 1919.

1921: ENGLISH ELECTRIC WREN

Acquired 1957

Span: 37 ft
Empty weight: 232 lb
Power: 398 cc A.B.C. horizontal twin

Although known mainly for its success in the Light Aeroplane Trials at Lympne, Kent, in 1923, the Wren flew two years before this when the first machine was built to Air Ministry order and serialled J6973. The idea was to produce an ultra-light training aeroplane of very low structure weight and capable of operating on very low power. Such a search for the ultimate in economy might seem more appropriate today, when we are faced with growing energy supply problems, but clearly cost was a hazard in the years shortly after the Great War.

The Wren's success at Lympne earned the type a lasting reputation, for in the trial one of the two contest machines flew 87.5 miles on one gallon of fuel, an achievement that it shared with the little ANEC monoplane, a dismantled specimen of which exists in the Collection. Clearly an aeroplane with such a small engine as that in the Wren would require all available power in order to achieve a sustained and positive climb, and there is no record of a Wren managing to fly higher than about 1200 feet. Overall performance was such that flights were

practical only in conditions of favourable wind and weather, so, along with other underpowered designs of the twenties, the Wren failed to attract a production order. Three Wrens were built, but mild confusion was caused by the constructor's numbers, which not only included a No. 4, but Nos. 3 and 4 flew with reversed identities, the first true civil registration not being allocated until 1926, when No. 4, flying as No. 3, became G-EBNV!

The Exhibit: Basically No. 4 (c/n 3) which was one of the Lympne machines, presented to the Collection by R H Grant of Dumfries; rebuilt by the English Electric Company by including many components from No. 3 (c/n 4) supplied by the Science Museum. Flown at Warton in January 1957 and handed-over at the Royal Aeronautical Society's Garden Party later that year. Extensively refurbished again at Warton in 1980 and returned to the Shuttleworth fleet early in 1981.

Although not flown conventionally since 30 April 1983, successful bungee launching trials were carried out in October 1992. Eleven people are needed for this operation, which has strong spectator appeal.

1923: DH 53 HUMMING BIRD Acquired 1954

Span: 30 ft 1 in
Empty weight: 326 lb
Power: 34 hp A.B.C. Scorpion horizontal twin
        (originally 750 cc Douglas)

The DH 53 was the first light aeroplane produced by the de Havilland Aircraft Company; two specimens were built in time for the famous *Daily Mail* light aeroplane trials at Lympne in 1923, at which the test pilot Hubert Broad impressed everyone present by performing loops and rolls on such a low-powered machine. This original 750 cc Douglas motorcycle engine, however, proved troublesome and all twelve production aircraft were fitted with 698 cc Blackburn Tomtit engines that developed 26 hp. Other engines used were the Bristol Cherub and A.B.C. Scorpion, both of which were horizontally-opposed two-cylinder units.

The DH 53 is thought of as a civil aeroplane, but after the two Lympne aircraft, the eight machines built for British use started their careers with the Royal Air Force, initially for evaluation as trainers and subsequently used on communications duties. Two were specially equipped for hooking trials with the airship R-33 and on 4 December 1925 the first release and re-engagement were successfully carried out with J 7325. Other DH 53s went abroad direct to civil customers; three to Australia, one to Czechoslovakia and the final example to Russia.

All eight RAF machines survived to be released in 1927, most to be put through the Royal Aircraft Establishment Aero Club at Farnborough for their Certificates of Airworthiness. Although too light and low-powered for popularity, with no production order for the British civil market, the ex-Service specimens flew for several years, the last, G-EBXN, passing through seven owners before being retired in 1938 and burned two years later.

The Exhibit: G-EBHX: One of the two original Lympne contestants. Found without engine in a shed near Deal in Kent by Squadron Leader L A Jackson, then the Collection's manager. Restored by the DH Technical School at Hatfield and fitted with A.B.C. Scorpion, to fly on 4 August 1960.

Following several in-flight engine stoppages, the last in August 1980, the DH 53 was grounded for research, engine rebuild and a new propeller. Also, with the sponsorship of Birmingham International Airport, which has the code BHX, some airframe modifications were carried out to improve historical accuracy, including fitting new, bigger wheels and corrections to wing shape. After taxying runs in April 1992, the first born-again flight was on 27 June. However, with a tank capacity of only 2¼ gallons, its activities are severely curtailed!

1924: DH 51

Acquired 1972

Span: 37 ft
Empty weight: 1342 lb
Power: 120 hp Airdisco 8-cylinder upright V
(originally 90 hp RAF 1a)

To present a guide in chronological order, the author faces several problems. Surely the DH 51 should appear before the DH 53? In practice the 51 flew ten months later than the 53 and this seems to be sufficient justification for the present arrangement.

Although the precise reason for the 51's late appearance is difficult to determine, the most likely cause was the lack of a suitable engine. War surplus 90 hp Royal Aircraft Factory (RAF) 1as were available and, although heavy and with only single ignition, one was fitted to the first machine of the type, G-EBIM, which flew in July 1924. However, the French Renault engine was being developed for civil use and, by fitting aluminium cylinder heads and other modifications, its output was increased from 80 to 120 hp to become the Airdisco. Remotored, 'IM flew again and obtained a C of A three months later.

The DH 51 was designed to accommodate two people and luggage, or three people, with a sliding top fuselage fairing to adjust the layout. Although well-liked and very docile, it proved rather large for the average owner's needs (which meant that hangarage was expensive) and only three were built. The first went to Australia and was converted to a seaplane, but capsized in Sydney harbour in 1931. The second was scrapped in 1933 and the third G-EBIR/VP-KAA became the first aircraft to be registered in Kenya, where it had an active existence lasting nearly forty years.

The Exhibit: G-EBIR (VP-KAA). The third and last built. Airfreighted from Nairobi to Hatfield in 1965 and restored by Hawker-Siddeley Aviation (now a part of British Aerospace) at Hawarden, Chester. Flown to Old Warden in 1972 to be placed in the permanent care of the Collection, where it operates as the only specimen of the oldest design of de Havilland origin to fly anywhere in the world. It is a key exhibit in the de Havilland range.

Late in 1987 'IR was repainted and some minor changes were made to ensure authenticity of detail.

1928: DH 60X MOTH

Acquired 1932

Span: 30 ft
Empty weight: 955 lb
Power: 105 hp Hermes II, 4-cylinder upright in-line
(originally 65 hp Cirrus I)

The DH 60 Moth must be considered as one of the most successful light aeroplanes of all time. Following the inadequacies of the diminutive DH 53 and the rather overweight DH 51, the Moth proved itself a winner from its first flight in February 1925. Apart from the rightness of the airframe design, the newly-available Cirrus engine provided both the required power output and the essential economy to go with it. This unit was developed by virtually cutting the eight cylinder Airdisco (see DH 51) in half, resulting in a four cylinder in-line that developed 60 hp for a weight of 290 lb.

The light aeroplane movement owes much of its growth to the introduction of the DH 60 and officialdom must have been less hidebound than it is today; by mid-1925 Sir Samuel Hoare, then Secretary of State for Air, became interested in its possibilities and the Air Ministry (in those days responsible for civil as well as military aviation) subsidized five flying clubs to be equipped with Moths: the Lancashire, London, Newcastle, Midland and Yorkshire.

Only three months after the first flight, Alan Cobham flew the prototype 1000 miles from Croydon to Zürich and back in a day and, by 1926, considerably more than half the aeroplanes attending flying meetings were Moths. Naturally the design was developed; an additional 25 hp was produced by the Cirrus II, with which many production machines were fitted. The Armstrong-Siddeley Genet five-cylinder radial engine was used by the RAF Central Flying School in six Moths that performed formation aerobatics at the 1927 Hendon display. In the next year, most production machines used the 90 hp Cirrus III, but a more notable improvement was the redesigned undercarriage of the split rather than straight-axle type, resulting in the designation DH 60X. This gave a smoother ride and was much more forgiving of misjudged landings!

A description of the slightly later DH 60G Gipsy Moth follows.

The Exhibit: G-EBWD. Built in 1928 and bought by Richard Shuttleworth at Brooklands in 1932, as his first aeroplane. Remotored from Cirrus II to Hermes in 1933. WD has lived at one aerodrome (Old Warden) for longer than any flying aeroplane in aviation history. This aeroplane has been sponsored by Tradition (UK) Group Ltd.

1928: DH 60G MOTH

Acquired 1977

Span: 30 ft
Empty weight: 920 lb
Power: 100 hp Gipsy I, 4-cylinder upright in-line
    (some with 120 hp Gipsy II)

By early 1928 the famous Gipsy engine had been designed by the de Havilland company and not surprisingly the first production units were earmarked for Moths. So the DH 60G Gipsy Moth was born as a logical successor to the already world-beating Cirrus variant.

One aim for headline hitting was to have the new machine ready for the 1928 King's Cup Air Race; this target was fulfilled, for fourteen Moths were entered and three of these were Gipsy-powered. One, G-EBYZ, became the winner after averaging a remarkable 105 mph round Britain. This was followed by many proving and publicity exercises: Captain Geoffrey de Havilland flew one to a record 21,000 ft and Hubert Broad remained airborne in another for twenty-four hours, but perhaps the most valuable achievement was an engine reliability trial, in which a production Gipsy I was sealed for 600 hours and required an expenditure on replacement parts of only £7.2.11 afterwards.

Gipsy Moths were exported in quantity and licence production was carried out in France, Australia and in the United States, while British-built machines held their heads high. Amy Johnson flew the famous *Jason*, G-AAAH (on display in the Science Museum) from Croydon to Darwin to become the first woman to fly from England to Australia. Francis Chichester achieved navigational fame when he found the diminutive Norfolk and Lord Howe islands in his float-fitted G-AAKK. John Grierson flew G-AAJP to Lahore, Baghdad, Moscow and Iceland. But we must not forget the hundreds of Gipsy Moths that provided popular and reliable mounts for private and club pilots of the thirties.

The Exhibit: G-ABAG. Constructor's No. 1259. Built 1930 and registered to Bentley Motors Ltd. Four subsequent pre-war owners; also loaned to the Stage and Screen Aero Club, during which time Ralph Richardson learnt to fly on it. Stored throughout 1939-45 war. Based at Perth from 1950 and subsequently owned alternatively by brothers Douglas and Peter Hull. Sold to, and crashed while in ownership of, Strathtay Aero Club and returned to Hull brothers. After Douglas Hull's death, his widow presented it to the Shuttleworth Collection, where it made its first public demonstration on 28 August 1977, prior to a formal hand-over on 13 October.

Repainted in original dark blue and silver colour scheme during winter of 1982-83.

1928: HAWKER TOMTIT   Acquired 1956

Span: 28 ft 6 in
Empty weight: 1100 lb
Power: 150 hp Armstrong-Siddeley Mongoose IIIc
        5-cylinder radial

As the Avro 504 series enjoyed such a long and successful career in the training role, the Royal Air Force had no requirement for a new trainer for twelve years after the end of World War I. In fact, very few new military aircraft of any type appeared during this quiet period in the twenties and the Tomtit was unusual in several ways. It was a completely new design, which became the first in the long line of Hawker military biplanes that were the mainstays of all but the heavy bomber and transport squadrons in the thirties. Although the better-known Hart light bomber flew first in prototype form, the Tomtit was ahead in initial issue to RAF units.

The Tomtit was one of the pace-setters in the change-over from wooden to metal construction, with a steel tube fuselage of a pattern that became the Hawker norm as far ahead as the Hurricane. Other salient features included wing slats, a blind-flying hood and a heavily staggered wing layout to permit rapid exit by parachute. There were no brakes, but the pupil's seat was adjustable for height. An unusual cockpit characteristic was the absence of a nut for adjusting throttle friction and yet the setting seemed to be suitable for all taxying and flight conditions.

In 1929 Tomtits were issued to No. 3 Flying Training School at Grantham (Spitalgate) and to the Central Flying School at Wittering. A Tomtit on the strength of No. 24 (Communications) Squadron at Northolt was flown regularly by the then Prince of Wales. The type was withdrawn from RAF service in 1935 and several were sold to civilian owners, to join a small number that had been built for the civil market and which did not see Service use. Tomtits were built also for the Royal Canadian and Royal New Zealand Air Forces.

The Tomtit is tail-light on the ground, but apart from a poor roll-rate with ailerons on the lower wings only, it is a delight to fly. Although a well-loved aeroplane among the relatively small number of sporting pilots who flew it in the thirties, a succession of entries in air races produced disappointing results.

Six Tomtits were flying at the outbreak of War in 1939 and all became camouflaged although, unusually, they remained civil registered for use on communications duties.

The Exhibit: K 1786/G-AFTA. The last Tomtit built and the only survivor. Flown as a 'hack' during World War II by Alex Henshaw of pre-war Mew Gull fame, who temporarily fitted a Spitfire windscreen. Later used by R G Stafford Allen, often for glider towing. Purchased by Neville Duke, then Hawkers' chief test pilot, who flew it in many races and displays. Purchased by Hawker Aircraft in 1950 to form the Hawker house trio (with the Hurricane and Hart), before hand-over to the Shuttleworth Collection in 1956. In 1967 it was repainted by Hawker-Siddeley at Dunsfold from a dark blue and gold scheme to its original Service markings.

Following a landing accident due to rough ground at Mildenhall in May 1985, there was considerable difficulty in obtaining correct engine/propeller harmonisation. Three propellers were made and tested, with much help from Dowty and Hoffman; eventually the latter firm designed a special high-rigidity propeller using composite woods and 'high-tech' covering. The Tomtit flew again on 25 June 1992.

1929: PARNALL ELF

Acquired 1951

Span: 31 ft 3 in
Empty weight: 1020 lb
Power: 105 hp Hermes II, 4-cylinder upright in-line

The Parnall Elf made its public debut at Olympia in July 1929. This was the last in a line of aeroplanes designed by Harold Bolas, most of which were built by George Parnall and Co of Yate, near Bristol — a carpentry firm that had turned over to aircraft production during the First World War. Previous Parnall machines included the Pixie, which along with many other ultra-light designs had achieved success in the 1923 Lympne trials and one version of which flew successfully as both a biplane and a monoplane; and the Imp, of 1927, which although fitted initially with an Armstrong-Siddeley Genet was used later for flight-testing the first of the Pobjoy radial engines.

The Elf was a two-seater biplane designed for the private and club market, with folding wings for storage economy and intended to require only minimum maintenance. The customary array of flying and landing wires could be dispensed with, as the interplane struts were arranged to form a Warren girder structure. Fuel was pumped from the main fuselage supply to a small header tank in the top wing centre section, from which the engine was gravity fed.

Three were built: G-AAFH, G-AAIN and G-AAIO. 'FH and 'IO were destroyed in flying accidents in 1934. In that year the last machine to carry the Parnall name — the Hendy Heck — first flew; a low wing cabin monoplane, it went into small-scale production and a little-known two-seat military trainer variant, the Heck 3, was remarkably similar in appearance to the better-known Miles Magister. Only one was constructed.

The Exhibit: G-AAIN. First flight June 1932. Owned by Lord Apsley at Badminton and stored throughout 1939-45 war. Based at Fairoaks and acquired by the Collection in non-flying condition in July 1951. Loaned for temporary static display to the Historic Aircraft Museum, Southend, in 1972. Subsequently fully restored at Old Warden by two former apprentices, to make its first public appearance in the air in August 1980.

Due to persistent magneto problems, the Elf was grounded during 1991-93. The magnetos appear to be susceptible to heat; currently a new type of internal insulation is being tried.

1929: SOUTHERN MARTLET

Acquired c. 1960

Span: 25 ft
Empty weight: 705 lb
Power: 100 hp Armstrong-Siddeley Genet Major
(but others used)

The origins of the Martlet stem from the Avro Baby, for in 1926 F G Miles, who had established Southern Aircraft at Shoreham in Sussex, acquired a number of main aircraft components from the former Avro factory at Hamble in Hampshire. Among these was a Baby, G-EAUM, which had been built as a two-seater in 1920. This machine, remotored with a 60 hp ADC Cirrus, providing twice the original power, had a lively performance which led to an order from L Bellairs for a single-seat aerobatic biplane. The basic design of the Avro Baby, with a new under-carriage and tail unit, became the Southern Martlet. The prototype, G-AAII, powered by an A.B.C. Hornet, was flown for the first time in August 1929 in the hands of F G Miles.

Altogether six Martlets were built, each different in one respect or another, as no fewer than five types of engine were used, while some had straight and others tapered ailerons. Although they were raced in several events, including the King's Cup, the results were generally disappointing. They achieved more success and popularity, though, as aerobatic and demonstration aeroplanes, serving with National Aviation Day Displays and C W A Scott's Air Display.

The sixth and last Martlet was completed at Shoreham in 1931, although a later variant, the Metal Martlet, appeared in that year. Only one was flown and this had a very short flying career.

The Exhibit: G-AAYX. For several years the personal mount of F G Miles, who took it with him to Woodley, near Reading, where Miles Hawks and later designs were built by Phillips and Powis Aircraft. This led to the type being called, incorrectly, the Miles Martlet. 'AYX survived World War II and was acquired by Butlins, who used it to give displays for holidaymakers at Broomhall, Pwllheli. Stored for more than 30 years before very extensive restoration to flying condition started in 1988.

1930: DH 80A PUSS MOTH Loaned since 1978, now by P & A Wood

Span: 36 ft 9 in
Empty weight: 1265 lb
Power: 130 hp Gipsy Major I inverted four-cylinder in-line
(at first 120 hp Gipsy III)

The open-cockpit Moths attracted many sporting pilots and their passengers, but some customers sought the comforts of the cabin, therefore removing the need to wear special flying clothing. To satisfy this demand, the de Havilland Aircraft Co produced the unnamed DH 80 high-wing enclosed tandem two-seater. A Gipsy II engine, which had been designed to run upright (with the cylinders pointing upwards) was modified to operate in the inverted attitude, which provides improved view for the pilot and a greater propeller ground clearance.

The DH 80 first flew in September 1929. Before production started, however, the original wooden fuselage structure was changed to one of welded steel tube; a door on the right side only was balanced by fitting one on each side and other refinements included an occasional third seat. The result was the DH 80A Puss Moth, which flew in March 1930.

Unfortunately Puss Moths and their occupants suffered serious accidents and several people were killed before the cause was discovered. By 1932, however, tests had proved that at high speed in turbulent conditions a wing failure could occur. Modifications included the addition of a small strut from the forward wing strut to the rear wing root fitting. Despite the bad start, the DH 80A became a popular and highly successful aeroplane with a number of achievements to its name; Australian-registered VH-UQO took third place in the handicap section of the England-to-Australia Air Race in 1934, averaging 103 mph, but perhaps the most noticeable performance was by Jim Mollison, who in 1933, flew G-ABXY from Lympne to Brazil to become the first person to fly from England to South America, and the first to make a solo east-west crossing of the South Atlantic.

Two hundred and fifty-nine Puss Moths were built between 1930 and 1933 and nearly half this number were exported.

The Exhibit: Exported new in 1931 as UN-PAX. Returned to England 1937 and registered G-AEOA. Impressed for RAF service during World War II as ES 921. Released 1946. Reconstructed while owned by Dr J H B Urmston in 1968. On long loan to the Collection since 1978.

1930: GRANGER ARCHAEOPTERYX

Acquired 1967

Span: 27 ft 6 in
Empty weight: 400 lb
Power: 32 hp Bristol Cherub flat twin

Between the wars many individuals and small companies designed and built ultra-light aeroplanes and, although few reached the production stage, many were interesting in concept. One such machine was the diminutive Archaeopteryx, which the brothers R F T and R J T Granger designed, with professional help from C H Latimer-Needham (designer of the Luton light aeroplanes, later the Halton Minor and others), after seeing the success of the Westland-Hill Pterodactyl in 1926. The result was a single-seater with swept-back wings and semi-tailless layout, in that it had a fin and rudder, but no tailplane or elevators. Full-chord elevons at the wingtips, hinged near the leading edge, provided control in both roll and pitch.

The Archaeopteryx flew at Hucknall, near Nottingham, in October 1930, but its identity belies its true age, for its registration G-ABXL was not issued until nearly two years later. Both Granger brothers flew their little machine many times locally in the Nottingham area and once ventured south as far as Hatfield for a flying display in June 1935. The throttle lever was on the outside of the fuselage, but performance on such low power depended very much on minimum exposed frontal area, and a positive rate of climb could be obtained only if the pilot's arms and elbows were tucked well into the cramped cockpit.

Tailless aeroplanes have always suffered aerodynamic problems with resulting control limitations and the Archaeopteryx must not be allowed to approach the stall. Another difficulty concerns the lack of fore-and-aft response in the take-off or landing stage, so any disturbance in pitch caused by rough ground or turbulence cannot be rectified and a landing bounce must lead to a series of bigger bounces until the airspeed decays and the aircraft stops. However, despite certain flight hazards, the idea and the design were most creditable. The Archaeopteryx was the first tractor (propeller in the front) tailless type and was a forerunner of the swept-wing machines in service today. Perhaps the recently-retired Vulcan heavy bomber is the best example.

The Exhibit: G-ABXL. The only specimen built. Flown 1930-36 and then stored for thirty years before hand-over to the Collection on 28 April 1967. Restored to flying condition in Old Warden workshops and flown again in June 1971.

Not currently flying due to aerodynamic problems related to tailless designs.

1931: DESOUTTER 1

Acquired 1935

Span: 36 ft
Empty weight: 1100 lb
Power: 115 hp Cirrus Hermes II

The Desoutter monoplane was built at Croydon, but apart from a few modifications was basically the Dutch-designed Koolhoven FK41. Although machines built on the continent appeared in this country from 1929, the forty-one produced in Britain emerged from the factory in the following two years. Nineteen of the type were acquired by National Flying Services for use on instructional, taxi and pleasure flying work. Two were owned by the British Red Cross Society and used for ambulance duties from Croydon and Woodford, while one was flown to New Zealand, where it continued in commercial service for twenty years. Another was used for joy riding and charter work in Northern Rhodesia. Richard Shuttleworth and his Warden Aviation Company owned three.

The Exhibit: G-AAPZ. Registered in 1931. Bought by Richard Shuttleworth in 1935 and modified with a Menasco C-4 Pirate engine. Flew briefly at Barton, Bedfordshire, during World War II. Exhibited at Hendon in 1951 and at Torbay in 1971. Subsequently housed at Old Warden until restoration started in 1985 by a volunteer team from the Shuttleworth Veteran Aeroplane Society.

1931: DH 82 TIGER MOTH   Acquired 1966

Span: 29 ft 4 in
Empty weight: 1090 lb
Power: Originally 120 hp DH Gipsy III, but later 130 hp
    Gipsy Major I, 4-cylinder inverted in-line

The DH 82 Tiger Moth is an earlier aeroplane than many people realize, for the prototype flew in October 1931. Although a few early production machines filtered from the factory at Stag Lane (later Hatfield) directly onto the civilian market, the majority served with the RAF or with the Elementary and Reserve Flying Schools; at that time, aircraft on these units carried civil registrations as they were owned by the companies that operated them under contract to the Air Ministry. In practice, therefore, the Tiger Moth was essentially an aeroplane earning its keep for Service purposes.

Developed from the DH 60 G Gipsy Moth, the DH 82 Tiger Moth was strengthened for Service use, incorporated an inverted rather than upright engine (which provided an improved forward view) and had the wings staggered for ease of exit by parachute. After initial experience with the type, the Air Ministry ordered several modifications, including the Gipsy Major engine instead of the Gipsy III and plywood instead of fabric-covered fuselage top decking. This became the DH 82 A Tiger Moth II, which remained the standard variant for the remainder of the type's history.

By 1937, spare production capacity enabled de Havilland to produce Tiger Moths in quantity for civil use. These were needed to replace a host of ageing types then in use with the flying clubs, but this was a relatively short lease of new life, for with war starting only two years later, all the machines on the lines were required for Service use. Then the Hatfield production facilities became fully committed to produce the Mosquito, so in 1941 Tiger Moth manufacture was transferred to Morris Motors at Cowley, near Oxford. In the same year, fuselage strakes were fitted to overcome difficulties with spin recovery.

Before, during and shortly after World War II the Tiger Moth was actively employed as the main elementary trainer for Service pilots. Nearly 7300 were built, including large numbers in Canada, Australia and New Zealand. Although replaced by Prentices in regular units by 1948, DH 82s continued to serve with Reserve Flying Schools and University Air Squadrons until superseded by Chipmunks in 1950-51. Since then, the Tiger Moth has remained a popular possession among sporting pilots and in recent years its market value has increased substantially; yet at the end of World War II, the Air Ministry disposed of hundreds in fly-away condition at £100 each, with a specially-arranged concession price of £50 if purchased by a recognized flying club. Some were sold for only £25 apiece.

The Tiger Moth was the last trainer to require pilots to fly in the traditional manner, taxying without the benefits of brakes, needing considerable use of rudder to maintain balanced flight, especially in turns, and generally flying largely by feel or, as it was termed 'by the seat of the pants'. Today three flying clubs operate DH 82 As, but only the Cambridge Flying Group provides basic instruction for beginners. Altogether about forty-five Tiger Moths are flying in Britain.

The Exhibit: T 6818/G-ANKT. Three Tiger Moths were acquired by the Collection in various states of disrepair, but the fuselage and most main components are from 'NKT. The rebuild was carried out almost entirely by two former engineering apprentices at Old Warden. First flight in Shuttleworth ownership was on 3 October 1977.

1931: AVRO TUTOR   Acquired 1959

Span: 34 ft
Empty weight: 1800 lb
Power: 240 hp. Armstrong-Siddeley Lynx IVc
         7-cylinder radial

The Tutor is difficult to date, for although the production version and the name appeared in 1931, a basically similar prototype known as the Avro Trainer, with an Armstrong-Siddeley Mongoose engine, had appeared in the new aircraft park at the RAF Pageant in 1930. A few Trainers served in the RAF for evaluation purposes alongside the similarly-powered Hawker Tomtit, but the later Lynx-engined Tutor became the standard production variant.

Tutors replaced Avro 504Ns at the Central Flying School, which worked-up an impressive formation aerobatic act with six aircraft that were painted with red and white stripes on the upper surfaces of the top wings to accentuate their inverted performances. From 1933 until 1936 this act became a regular and much-admired feature of the Hendon Displays. On more routine duties Tutors served with the Royal Air Force College at Cranwell and with Nos. 3 and 5 Flying Training Schools at Grantham and Sealand respectively. At Grantham, the type replaced Tiger Moths, which surprisingly had entered service a short time previously as 504N replacements.

The Tutor was a luxurious and well-equipped aeroplane for its time, with a tailwheel, effective brakes, seats that could be adjusted for height and rudder pedals for distance, unusually spacious cockpits and a variable incidence tailplane. With ailerons on upper and lower wings, control was positive with good roll response. Perhaps it was a little docile as a trainer; certainly it required less attention to detail than the Tiger Moth, although the Tutor's large radial engine must have been useful as an exercise in teaching the operation of more powerful motors.

In addition to the standard production machines, between 1934 and 1936 fourteen Tutors were produced as floatplanes for use by the Seaplane Training Flight at Calshot and a developed Tutor variant, the Avro 626, entered service in small numbers in 1935 with the Air Navigation School at Andover. This was given the name Prefect and although civil 626s retained the Lynx engine, those for the RAF were fitted with 277 hp Cheetahs.

Primarily a military aeroplane, only nineteen Tutors appeared on the civil register and three were equipped with survey cameras to map large areas of Tanganyika. The type was used also by Air Service Training at Hamble. Of the later 626 and 637 variants, seventeen held British registrations and several were exported to Hong Kong.

Three ex-RAF Tutors survived World War II, but by 1949 one had succumbed to the effects of age and another was lost in an accident following an engine failure.

The Exhibit: K3215/G-AHSA. The sole surviving Tutor. One of the main RAF production batch built in 1933. Served with the RAF College, Cranwell, 1933-36 and then with the Central Flying School. Later used on communications duties and believed to be the last Tutor on RAF strength when struck-off as late as December 1946. It was 'demobbed' at Weston-super-Mare and subsequently owned by John Neasham of Darlington & District Aero Club. Later privately owned at Burnaston, Derby, by Wing Commander Heywood, it suffered crankshaft failure on a ground-run for the film *Reach for the Sky*, when it was purchased by the Collection. The engine subsequently used was built-up by Armstrong-Siddeley at Coventry from the best components of three non-working units including one in the museum of the College of Aeronautics at Cranfield. Engine problems in 1979 caused the machine to be grounded for a considerable time, but as a world-wide search failed to find a suitable Lynx engine, the existing one was painstakingly rebuilt at Old Warden in 1981-82 by a senior member of the engineering staff.

1932: ARROW ACTIVE MK II Loaned 1982

Span: 24 ft
Empty weight: 925 lb
Power: 120 hp Gipsy III, 4-cylinder inverted in-line

The Arrow Aircraft Company of Leeds, under the design leadership of Arthur Thornton, designed and built two Actives. The first, G-ABIX, powered by a 115 hp Cirrus Hermes IIB, first flew at Sherburn-in-Elmet and was issued with a Certificate of Airworthiness on 21 May 1931.

Judged 'fast, though tricky' it was unplaced in the 1932 and 1933 King's Cup Air Race and was later purchased by Alex Henshaw. On 30 December 1935, whilst practising high 'G' inverted aerobatics, the engine burst into flames and Henshaw was forced to bale out, 'BIX being totally destroyed in the ensuing crash.

The sole Active II with its Gipsy III engine appeared in 1932 and was described by the makers as 'representing to a proportionately smaller scale all the features of construction and performance found in the latest types of single-seater, high performance Service aircraft'.

Intended for advanced flight training and competition, the Active II was raced in 1932 and '33 with little success. With no orders forthcoming, Arrow Aircraft diversified from aircraft production and in 1935 this aesthetically pleasing and, for its day, advanced aircraft was laid up.

The Exhibit: G-ABVE. Constructor's No. 2. Built in 1932 and participated in 1932 and 1933 King's Cup Air Race.

Stored from 1935 to 1957 'BVE was then reconditioned with a 145 hp Gipsy Major 1C for use by the Tiger Club. Purchased by Desmond Penrose in 1979, this unique aircraft was placed second in the 1980 King's Cup.

Detailed restoration to original specification started in 1981, with reversion to a Gipsy III engine being completed in April 1989.

1933: FLYING FLEA

Acquired 1967

Span: 20 ft
Empty weight: 220 lb
Power: Various, including Scott, Carden-Ford, Douglas
     Sprite, A.B.C. Scorpion and Bristol Cherub

The Flying Flea was not intended to be a factory-produced aeroplane, for its French designer, M. Henri Mignet, aimed at the do-it-yourself market, which, though popular today in many spheres, is far from a new idea. The Flea's French name was Pou-de-Ciel, which translated literally into Sky Louse.

M. Mignet endeavoured to remove the characteristics of a conventional light aeroplane that were likely to be dangerous in the hands of a novice pilot who had just built his own machine. Throughout the era of flight, stalling and spinning had proved to be hazardous unknowns, so he aimed to reduce the need for control movements to an absolute minimum. By giving the wings considerable dihedral (upward curve) and placing the weight well beneath them, he dispensed with ailerons, relying wholly on pendulum stability to maintain lateral control. Fore-and-aft movement was achieved by hinging the front wing at its leading edge, so that fore-and-aft adjustment of the joystick altered the angle of incidence. There was no form of movement and no hinged surface on the rear wing or tailplane.

Although many pilots and engineers were sceptical about the practicability of these ideas, M. Mignet brought his machine to Shoreham in Sussex in August 1935 and many people were highly impressed by its apparent success. The Air League took the Flea into the fold and encouraged the formation of Pou Clubs. Six thousand copies of the designer's handbook were printed in English and by 1937 nearly 100 Fleas had been registered in Britain.

Unfortunately, after a bright start, the Flea ran into control problems and some of these developed into fatal accidents. The Air League recommended that the type should not be flown until the difficulties had been identified and cured; following this, full-scale wind tunnel tests at Farnborough and in France indicated several serious shortcomings, with the result that the Flea failed to recover from this setback. The designer, however, insisted that the idea was sound and he developed a slightly more advanced version which flew successfully in limited numbers. One of these was built in Britain shortly after World War II.

The Exhibit: G-AEBB. Registered 1937. Early history not confirmed, but for several years after the war, was in the care of No. 124 (Southampton) Squadron of the Air Training Corps. The squadron donated it to the Collection in May 1967, since when it has been restored by A Dowson (*see* Swallow) of the SVAS. Although technically airworthy, the Flea is not flown, but occasionally is taxied on public occasions.

1933: CIERVA C.30A
1934: AVRO ROTA

Acquired 1954

Rotor diameter: 37 ft
Empty weight: 1270 lb
Power: 140 hp Armstrong-Siddeley Genet Major 1A
      7-cylinder radial

Don Juan de la Cierva, who is credited with inventing the first practical rotating wing, brought his first autogiro to the UK from his native Spain in 1925 at the invitation of the Air Ministry. This, the C.6A, was basically an Avro 504K without its mainplanes and fitted with a four-bladed rotor on a steel tube pylon. A developed version, the C.6D, still based on the 504, became the first two-seat autogiro, flying for the first time from Hamble in July 1926.

The rotors on Cierva's machines were not driven by or connected to the engine, but relied for their rotation wholly on a forward airspeed; hence the name autogiro. Not surprisingly there were many development problems and a number of crashes, but each difficulty was thoroughly investigated and a long research programme continued; during this time various one-off variants were produced to Cierva's designs by the A V Roe, de Havilland and Comper companies, with a production batch of fifteen C.19s built at Hamble. The Autogiro Flying School operated from Hanworth, now swamped in the empire known as London Airport (Heathrow).

The autogiro came into its own with the design of the C.30A. The earlier machines had used movable flying control surfaces on the same principle as a conventional aeroplane, the C.19 having ailerons, elevator and rudders. This had resulted in the benefits of the inherent slow flying qualities, with scope for nearly vertical landing approaches, to be largely negated because these controls became progessively less effective as airspeed decreased. With the C.30A, however, a tilting rotor head with a control column hanging down from it provided control movements in all three axes; when the column was moved sideways for a turn, the machine assumed the correct bank angle.

By this time the Royal Air Force was interested in the use of the autogiro for army co-operation duties. Between August 1934 and May 1935, twelve Cierva C.30As, known as the Avro Rota, were built for the Service under contract by A V Roe and Co Ltd at Manchester and were based initially at Old Sarum. With the outbreak of war in 1939, these Rotas were joined by a number of impressed civil C.30As, the type serving briefly at Duxford, and later at Halton and Henley. No. 529 Squadron was the only full autogiro squadron in the RAF, but the Rotas remained in use until the end of hostilities in 1945 when the unit was disbanded.

Twelve Cierva C.30As survived the war for sale as surplus at RAF Kemble, but few were used again to any extent, although the Fairey Aviation Company operated three for brief experiments and to gain rotary-wing experience while building the prototype Fairey Gyrodyne helicopter. The last airworthy specimen, G-AHTZ (which had been G-ACUI before the war, HM 581 in wartime, and should have been re-issued with its original registration) was burned in an accident at Elmdon Airport, Birmingham, in 1958.

The Exhibit: K4235/G-AHMJ. Built as an Avro Rota for the RAF in 1934. One of six purchased by Richard Shuttleworth by tender at Cardington (but without engines) shortly before World War II as surplus to Service needs. Stored at Old Warden until impressed for further Service use and taken to Duxford on 3 May 1941, when total time flown since new was only 108 hours. Subsequently released again and registered to Fairey Aviation in 1946, but disposed of a year later to Hayes & Harlington Sea Cadets. Transferred to Shuttleworth Collection in 1954, stored for many years and subsequently restored by SVAS member Ken Hyde and partner. Loaned to the Army Air Corps Museum during 1982. Following overhaul of engine and magnetos, fired-up and taxied for first time in 45 years on 13 July 1992. Several items obtained from RAF Cardington to be incorporated into the airframe and rotor-head, to enable the rotor to turn safely on the chocks.

1934: DH 87b HORNET MOTH Acquired 1971

Span: 31 ft 11 in
Empty weight: 1241 lb
Power: 130 hp Gipsy Major I, 4-cylinder inverted in-line

The Hornet Moth emerged in 1934 as an experimental design in an attempt to find the pattern for a modernized version of the original DH 60 Moth series. Clearly an enclosed cabin would be incorporated and side-by-side seating seemed sensible for a 'social' aeroplane. At first the DH 87 had tapered wings with almost pointed tips; these were similar to those on the DH 86 four-engined airliner that had been its immediate predecessor. Three Hornet Moths were used in a (for that time) extended testing programme lasting for a year before quantity production began.

The first batch for sale was completed in August 1935 and altogether 165 were built. However, during the development process a new, squarer wing design appeared and owners of early machines were invited to trade-in their original mainplanes for those of later layout. The change was made in order to eliminate a tendency for a wing to drop at low speed, which was considered to be an unacceptable characteristic on a machine aimed mainly at the private-owner market. The revised version was designated DH 87b and before long all the UK-based pointed-wing specimens had disappeared.

Unlike many de Havilland designs, the Hornet Moth was not a top-line record breaker, but a comfortable mount for the executive of the day. However, it appeared in all parts of the world and examples were assembled in South Africa, Canada, Australia and India. Four were equipped with floats for Air Ministry seaplane trials at Felixstowe.

The DH 87b was less of a 'pilots aeroplane' than many de Havilland products, but it offered a good forward view, plenty of comfort and a useful range of more than 600 miles. As with the Puss Moth, the undercarriage leg fairings could be turned through ninety degrees to act as air brakes. About eight Hornet Moths remain active today.

The Exhibit: G-ADND. Now powered by 145 hp Gipsy Major 10. Owned for many years by P Q Reiss who on retirement passed it to the Air Registration Board (predecessor of today's Airworthiness Division of the CAA). Following an accident, Mr Reiss transferred it to the Shuttleworth Collection, for whom it was rebuilt by Hawker Siddeley/British Aerospace at Chester.

1934: DH 88 COMET

Acquired 1965

Span: 44 ft
Empty weight: 2840 lb
Power: 2 x 230 hp Gipsy Six R high-compression
6-cylinder inverted in-line (but see text)

If any historic aeroplane has received well-earned publicity in recent years, perhaps the de Havilland Comet of 1934 takes the lead, but this is not its first round of headline-hitting. The DH 88 was designed, built and flown in a total time of nine months to enter and win the MacRobertson Air Race in October of the same year.

That simple statement in no way expresses the magnitude of the tasks; either of producing an aeroplane with so many novel features such as unique wooden stressed-skin construction, two-pitch propellers, a retractable undercarriage and a range of 2900 miles from tanks contained wholly within the slender fuselage, all in such record time; or of restoring a complex and incomplete aeroplane to fly again after more than forty-three years on the ground in a wide range of storage conditions.

The Comet story starts with an offer — or a challenge — from Sir MacPherson Robertson, who put up £10,000 in prize money for a race from England to Australia to mark the centenary of the foundation of the State of Victoria. Most entrants planned to compete in existing aircraft types and only one company — de Havilland — was sufficiently enterprising to make positive proposals for a new design solely for the race. DH offered to produce the Comet at a highly subsidized price of £5,000 for each aircraft, on condition that orders were confirmed by February 1934. In the event, three orders were received, and, by constant work day and night, the company had all three machines ready just in time to be tested and handed over prior to the deadline for appearing at the start-line at Mildenhall.

To achieve high speed, long range and accommodate a crew of two, the Comet called for considerable design ingenuity. Very clean aerodynamic lines were essential, with an absolute minimum of frontal area. To obtain both the required smoothness of form and an adequately robust structure, much of the strength was contained in the skin, which for the wings and upper and lower surfaces of the fuselage consisted of diagonally placed spruce strips. On the wings these strips, which ran at forty-five degrees to the fore and aft axis of the aircraft, were of equal width throughout but were tapered in thickness from root to tip.

Fortunately engines of the desired size and weight were available from within the de Havilland organization. The 205 hp Gipsy Six had all six cylinders in a line and therefore offered a small frontal area, but as maximum possible power was required the basic unit was modified with an increased compression ratio and a consequent

reduction in depth of the cylinder heads, therefore providing an additional 25 hp and an ability to fit tightly into small cowlings. However, in order to take off with heavy fuel loads from small airfields and yet cruise economically at the high end of the speed range, the available engine power could not be fully used with the existing patterns of propellers of fixed pitch design. Ratier, of France, had produced two-pitch propellers — fine for take-off and coarse for cruise — and these were used, although the pitch settings were not controllable from the cockpit. A bicycle pump was used to establish the fine setting before starting the engines; discs in the propeller hubs were designed to respond to air pressure when the aircraft accelerated through 140 mph after take-off, releasing the pumped-up air pressure and causing centrifugal weights to put the propellers into fully coarse pitch with a clunk. It is interesting to wonder whether both sides changed pitch at the same time!

The air race was scheduled to start at dawn on 20 October 1934. On the line at the new RAF station at Mildenhall, a host of competing types ranged from the new Douglas DC-2 and Boeing 247 airliners to a Miles Hawk from the Manawatu Aero Club of New Zealand. The three Comets were there; the black and gold G-ACSP, called *Black Magic*, owned and entered by the already famous Jim and Amy Mollison; G-ACSR, unnamed, but painted green, owned by Bernard Rubin who had engaged Owen Cathcart-Jones and Ken Waller to be his race pilots; and G-ACSS, red and white (although recently discovered DH workshop notes indicate that the white might have been silver), known as *Grosvenor House* and entered by A O Edwards who was the hotel's managing director. The pilots for this were C W A Scott and Tom Campbell-Black.

The story of the race warrants a book of its own. *Black Magic* and *Grosvenor House* each reached Baghdad non-stop, but the nameless 'SR had compass and other problems in very bad weather and the pilots were forced to make an unscheduled landing in Persia. En route, though, the fortunes changed, with 'SP retiring through repeated engine trouble; 'SR was in business again and making fast headway, but *Grosvenor House* was just in the lead, with the KLM (Royal Dutch Airlines) DC-2 too close behind for crew comfort. All participants endured a variety of weather and technical problems, but after seventy hours and fifty-four minutes, G-ACSS *Grosvenor House* was the first to cross the finishing line. The Comet qualified for both main prizes — one for speed and one for

handicap — but the race rules prevented both awards going to one competitor, so the crew of 'SS opted for the main (speed) prize and the other trophy was presented to the crew of the DC-2.

The Comet was a thoroughbred aeroplane, designed and built for one purpose: to travel a long way in a short time. G-ACSR, which had finished fourth, turned around almost immediately, loaded with newsreels, photographs of the winners and other valuable booty, to arrive at Lympne in Kent thirteen-and-a-half days after leaving Mildenhall, thus establishing an out-and-return record. G-ACSS, however, had a more leisurely journey home on board a ship; but its flying days were far from finished. As the Comet was such an advanced design, 'SS temporarily lost its bright civil colours to become K 5084 in the Royal Air Force for trials at Marlesham Heath; as such it appeared in the 1936 Pageant at Hendon. However, following a second landing accident whilst in RAF service, it was sold as scrap, to be bought by F E Tasker who had it rebuilt by Essex Aero Ltd at Gravesend, where the exceptionally skilled engineer Jack Cross worked wonders both then and later, for Mr Cross was actively helping with the restoration of 'SS at Old Warden until he died towards the end of 1981.

In its new ownership G-ACSS was renamed *The Orphan* and gained fourth place in the England to Damascus race of 1937; later in that year the same stalwart, by then called *The Burberry* (of raincoat renown) beat the out-and-back record to the Cape, but its final achievement was in March 1938 when it covered the 26,450 miles from England to New Zealand and home again in only ten days, twenty-one hours and twenty-two minutes. From then on, 'SS was stored at Gravesend, where it passed much of World War II standing forlornly outside.

In addition to the three MacRobertson race participants, two later Comets were built. G-ACSP had been sold to the French Government to become F-ANPY, to be joined by a new F-ANPZ for use on high-speed mail services. The final DH 88 to leave the Hatfield factory was lost over the Sudan when the crew baled out with serious propeller problems in an attempt on the Cape record.

The Exhibit: G-ACSS. Early history already described. After the war years at Gravesend, restored externally by de Havilland apprentices, to be hung on exhibition in the Festival of Britain in 1951. Subsequently stored at Leavesden before hand-over as a static exhibit for the Shuttleworth Collection on 30 October 1965. In the early seventies, plans were considered for restoring this famous aeroplane to fly again; despite many problems a decision was made to go ahead to rebuild this famous aeroplane for the nation on the understanding that it would not drain the Collection's financial resources. An appeal was launched, with the Transport Trust and Hawker Siddeley Aviation making substantial launching grants. Initial work was carried out at Old Warden and about fifty organisations in the aviation and allied industries supported the project either technically or financially, but more extensive base facilities were required. Work was transferred initially to the Royal Aircraft Establishment at Farnborough and finally to British Aerospace at Hatfield, where it flew again for the first time in forty-nine years on Sunday 17 May 1987. First appearance at an Old Warden display was on 31 May. Due to problems with cross-wind operations from today's hard runways and a landing incident that caused some damage, modifications were incorporated including a lockable tailwheel. Flew again on Friday 26 August 1988, and in September appeared at the Farnborough display and the Shuttleworth 60th anniversary Pageant. A popular performer.

1934: HAWKER HIND

Acquired 1971

Span: 37 ft 3 in
Empty weight: 3250 lb
Power: 640 hp Rolls-Royce Kestrel V 12-cylinder
      liquid-cooled Vee

Without the long line of Hawker military biplanes that served in the thirties, the backbone of the Royal Air Force would have been very thin. With the ubiquitous Hart and its descendants fulfilling almost every role in almost every sphere, the Fury as a single-seat fighter, the Demon as a two-seat fighter, the Audax on army co-operation, the Hardy on general duties and the Hind as an all-purpose day bomber, all were powered by various versions of the Rolls-Royce Kestrel and all were broadly similar in appearance. Of all the Hawker types of the period that served with the RAF only the first — the relatively small Tomtit trainer of 1928 — and the last — the Hector of 1936 which was an Audax replacement — were powered by engines other than the Kestrel.

The Hind entered the arena when the Hawker biplane series was well matured and in the early days of the RAF's pre-war expansion scheme. The prototype took to the air on 12 September 1934 and the first production machine for No. 21 squadron at Bircham Newton, flew almost exactly a year later. Altogether 528 Hinds were built and these replaced Harts on nearly all first-line light bomber units, as well as forming the equipment for several new squadrons in a rapidly-growing air force.

The Hind differed from its predecessor in having more than 100 additional hp from its supercharged Kestrel, a tailwheel in place of a skid (although later Hart Trainers had wheels), a more developed exhaust system and a cut-away rear cockpit to provide a better view for the gunner.

The last Hinds were replaced in front-line squadrons in the UK shortly before the start of World War II, but about 140 were converted — and twenty built — as dual-control advanced trainers to join and sometimes replace the 500 Hart trainers that had been supplied previously; some of these served into the early forties. The author remembers seeing six of these aircraft, camouflaged, of course, by contrast with the pre-war silver finish, operated by the Air Transport Auxiliary at White Waltham as late as 1942. They were hidden in an orchard and taxied across a road to the aerodrome before and after flight. Overseas, Hart variants were used in many places and in many roles, especially on the north-west frontier in India, with two batches of Hinds delivered to the Royal Afghan Air Force: the first with eight new aircraft in 1938 and two years later ten ex-RAF machines. Almost certainly the last of the Hart variants to serve in Britain in numbers (although a few odd specimens survived as 'hacks') were Hectors used for towing Hotspur training gliders. The last few of these were

withdrawn and replaced by Masters early in 1943. The Afghans, however, continued to operate their Hinds until 1956.

The Exhibit: One of the machines delivered new to the Royal Afghan Air Force in 1938. Presented to the Shuttleworth Collection and retrieved overland on a journey of 6000 miles with transport supplied by the Ford Motor Company. Subsequently restored in the Old Warden workshops to fly for the first time in a quarter of a century on 17 August 1981. Made its first public appearance in the air, resplendent in Afghan markings, on 25 October 1981. Later repainted in the markings of 15 Squadron Royal Air Force, as K5414, and now one of the most popular performers in the Collection.

In 1987-88 the Kestrel engine was overhauled with sponsorship from Aero Vintage Ltd.

1935: B.A. SWALLOW 2

Loaned by
Tony Dowson
since 1978

Span: 42 ft 8½ in
Empty weight: 990 lb
Power: 90 hp Pobjoy Cataract III 7-cylinder radial
    (some had 90 hp Cirrus Minor 4-cylinder in-line)

In 1927 the Klemm L 25 two-seat low-wing monoplane appeared in Germany as a safe and comfortable mount for private owners. Despite its Salmson radial engine of only 75 hp, the type proved popular immediately and soon specimens were delivered to Britain.

The L 25 owed its success to a low wing-loading, docile handling qualities and a reliable engine. By 1933 Major E F Stephen, the UK agent, had imported and sold twenty-seven aircraft before establishing the British Klemm Aeroplane Company to build these machines at Hanworth. The British-built version differed little from the German original, but the airframe was strengthened in a few parts and after the first six machines, the production power unit was changed from the Salmson to the Pobjoy Cataract, which offered an additional 15 hp. By 1935, however, some redesign work had been completed, to square-off the wing-tips, rudder, tailplane and fuselage top-decking for ease of quantity construction; the result became known as Swallow 2. New finance was injected into the business and the UK firm became the British Aircraft Manufacturing Company.

The 42nd airframe to be built in Britain used the Blackburn Cirrus Minor four-cylinder inverted in-line engine and, from that point onwards, a roughly equal number of Swallows left the line with this and with the Cataract. These aircraft were built essentially for the British home market, for ninety-eight out of 105 produced at Hanworth were acquired by flying clubs or private owners in this country. Not surprisingly, a leading user of the Cirrus-powered Swallow was the Blackburn Aircraft Co, which operated fifteen on No. 4 Elementary and Reserve Flying School at Brough in East Yorkshire.

Unlike many civil light aircraft in common use in the late thirties, in general Swallows were not impressed into active flying service in World War II. One flew as a glider at Farnborough, but the majority suffered the relative indignity of being used as ground instructional airframes. Despite (or perhaps because of) this, seventeen Swallow 2s survived to fly again shortly after the war. Today one Klemm L 25 and two B.A. Swallows remain in flying condition.

The uncowled radial is heavily geared-down between the engine and propeller and the sound is unmistakable.

The Exhibit: G-AFCL. Built November 1937 and registered to W L Hope. Owned immediately after World War II by G H Forsaith, who based it at Thruxton. To Bert Etheridge (wood craftsman at Old Warden) in May 1965. Owned and restored for the Collection by A Dowson, a member of the Shuttleworth Veteran Aeroplane Society.

1935: PERCIVAL D.3 GULL-SIX

Acquired 1961

Span: 36 ft 2 in
Empty weight: 1500 lb
Power: 200 hp Gipsy Six I, 6-cylinder inverted in-line

The Gull is an example of an aeroplane that is difficult to date, for the original machine that flew first in 1932 was a substantially different aircraft from the variant that emerged two years later. The earlier version was built under contract by George Parnall and Co Ltd of Yate, near Bristol (see Parnall Elf) and this had either the 160 hp Napier Javelin or 130 hp Gipsy Major as a power source. By 1934, however, the Percival Aircraft Co Ltd had its own factory at Gravesend and from here the design developed with a neater, single-strut undercarriage and eventually boasted the additional performance offered by the 200 hp Gipsy Six engine. The exhibit in the Collection is one of these later machines, built in 1935.

As with all Percival aircraft of the time, the Gull range was designed by and built under the supervision of Edgar Percival, who carried out the first flight of the prototype in 1932 and flew it in the King's Cup Air Race of that same year. At one stage the company used a series of type numbers that continued into the post-war era of the Provost, Prince and Pembroke, but these had been retrospectively allocated to the machines of the thirties and a 'P' designation was wrongly attributed to the Gull-Six.

An early Gull-Four flew from Lympne in Kent to Darwin, Australia, in the hands of Sir Charles Kingsford Smith, to arrive on 10 December 1933 after seven days, four hours and forty-four minutes. In 1935, Edgar Percival flew a Gull-Six from Gravesend to Algeria and back in a day, while shortly afterwards Jean Batten began her series of record-breaking activities, starting with the first flight across the South Atlantic by a woman pilot that enabled her to reach Brazil in two days, thirteen hours and fifteen minutes after leaving Lympne. For this she was awarded the CBE. In the following year she set course for Australia and reached Darwin from England in five days, twenty-one hours and three minutes. She extended this to complete the first-ever flight from England to New Zealand. The return flight from Darwin to Lympne was achieved in two hours forty-eight minutes less than on the outward journey.

The basic Gull was developed into the more sophisticated four-seat Vega Gull, which in turn formed the basis for the Percival Proctor of RAF radio-training and communications renown. One other Gull-Six and three Proctors remain in flying condition.

The Exhibit: G-ADPR. Built September 1935. The machine was used by Jean Batten for all her record flights. Impressed into wartime RAF service as AX 866 and later bought back by the Percival Aircraft Co Ltd, whose Directors (by then Hunting Percival) passed it to the Collection on 25 April 1961. The subject of a major rebuild, sponsored by Hunting Engineering, in 1988-1989.

Some of the work sub-contracted to Hants Light Plane Services. Flown again in May 1990, but dismantled to fly aboard a Boeing 747 to Auckland International Airport in July, for display during the 150th anniversary of the foundation of New Zealand. It returned in April 1991 and flew again in the following month.

1935: GLOSTER GLADIATOR Acquired 1960

Span: 32 ft 3 in
Empty weight: 3450 lb
Power: 840 hp Bristol Mercury 9-cylinder radial

The Gladiator was the last in the line of inter-war Gloster fighters — following the Grebe, Gamecock and Gauntlet — to become the RAF's final biplane fighter. The type started as an unnamed private venture and in this form flew as early as September 1934, to be followed by an order for twenty-three aircraft placed in July of the following year. The machines ordered for RAF service differed from the earlier prototype in having enclosed cockpits with sliding hoods and a more developed mark of Mercury engine.

In its production form, to Air Ministry specification 14/35, the Gladiator entered front-line service with No. 72 Squadron in February 1937 and with No. 3 Squadron a month later. Before the initial deliveries were made, a further 180 had been ordered and success was such that manufacture continued until April 1940, by which time nearly 500 had been built for British use and about 240 had been delivered to nine overseas air forces.

The Gladiator was both the last of the old and the first of the new. By the late thirties, a biplane with a fixed undercarriage had a short life expectation as an operational aeroplane, but the enclosed cockpit, flaps and four .303in Browning machine guns providing twice the fire power of its predecessors gave it a logical place in the move towards the monoplane. Clearly Gladiators were obsolescent as fighters by the beginning of World War II, but they served gallantly in many spheres and formed the equipment of No. 247 Squadron to defend the naval dockyard at Plymouth in the Battle of Britain. Their most publicly-acclaimed wartime exploits were the operations from a frozen lake in Norway and in the defence of Malta, but later they continued to serve in small numbers on line duties, particularly on meteorological reconnaissance work. The author remembers seeing a camouflaged Gladiator at White Waltham and another visiting Hawkers' airfield at Langley as late as the end of 1944.

With 253 mph as its published top speed (always a design figure that eludes anyone who flies any type) the Gladiator depended mainly on its impressive manoeuvrability to succeed operationally; certainly in an unhostile environment that enables the lone cockpit occupant to enjoy the pure pleasures of flight, the Gladiator excelled as a flying machine and those of us who have been privileged to take the air in the Collection's preserved specimen will not forget either its impressive handling features or the associated atmosphere that provides such ample scope for an imaginative mind.

The Exhibit: L8032/G-AMRK. Manufactured in 1938. The world's only airworthy Gladiator. Built-up to flying condition in 1948 by Vivian Bellamy at Eastleigh, Southampton and flown under civil markings. Passed to the Gloster Aircraft Company and extensively rebuilt at Hucclecote during the early fifties; guns were fitted and the aircraft was repainted in Service markings. When Gloster Aircraft closed down, was presented by Hawker Siddeley to the Collection for safe keeping in November 1960. For a time it flew with the incorrect serial K8032 to represent a machine on the strength of No. 72 Squadron. A second, incomplete Gladiator (parts of which were used in the original post-war rebuild) is owned by the Collection and is on long loan to the Royal Naval Air Station at Yeovilton, Somerset, where it is exhibited in the Fleet Air Arm Museum.

In May 1990, L8032 was repainted in camouflage scheme with markings of No 247 Squadron to mark 50th anniversary of the Battle of Britain, when the unit operated the type from Roborough, Plymouth. A persistent problem for many years has been a fruitless search for a serviceable exhaust collector ring. L8032's flying career has been helped through sponsorship by Luton International Airport.

1937: MILES M.14 A MAGISTER

Acquired 1970

Span: 33 ft 10 in
Empty weight: 1286 lb
Power: 130 hp DH Gipsy Major I, 4-cylinder inverted in-line

The Miles Magister, as the first monoplane trainer to be ordered for service with the Royal Air Force, owed its existence to the series of civil Hawks designed by F G Miles, the first of which, the M.2, flew from Woodley, near Reading in March 1933. Because a supply of Cirrus engines had been obtained at give-away prices from a company that had gone into liquidation, the Hawk was able to penetrate the private owner market very effectively at an ex-factory price of only £395! The design was developed, not surprisingly to become powered by the ubiquitous de Havilland Gipsy Major, and the first M.2F Hawk Major (temporarily cleaned-up as a single-seater) gained second place in the King's Cup Air Race of 1934 at 147 mph. From then on, the long line of Miles low-wing monoplanes developed at a fast pace.

Before the all-wood M.14A Magister entered service, to specification T40/36, a Hawk Major had been delivered to the RAF in 1936 and thirteen Hawk Trainers (progressively modified Majors) were used by the new Elementary and Reserve Flying Training School at Woodley. The more robust 'Maggie', though, joined the Service in September 1937 with the delivery of L5913 to the Central Flying School. Subsequently 1242 were built for the RAF and these served with no fewer than sixteen Elementary Flying Training Schools. Unlike the Tiger Moth, which continued in military use for a further six years, the Magister was declared obsolete at the end of the war, although the author remembers one lone camouflaged specimen among the Tigers at No. 3 EFTS, Shellingford, in May 1947.

The idea behind the Magister was to provide a trainer with a configuration closely related to the many operational monoplanes that were entering the RAF in the late thirties. A low wing setting, vacuum-operated split trailing edge flaps, a meaningful stall and a requirement for very positive action to effect spin recovery (later softened slightly with the introduction of fuselage strakes) provided the Service with an elementary trainer geared to the needs of the time. Although in the early stages some pupils reverted to the biplane for advanced tuition on the Hart or Hind trainer, the majority progressed to more powerful monoplanes such as the Miles Master or, later, the North American Harvard. Many who were destined to fly twin-engined aircraft moved on to the Airspeed Oxford. From the aspect of acquiring handling skills, there could be no better training combinations.

After the war, no fewer than 148 Magisters were released from RAF use and became registered under the civil name of Hawk Trainer III. The type achieved success in the air racing field, cleaned-up in a number of ways, including neat conversions to single-seaters and taping the gaps between the wings and ailerons. Several were used by flying clubs for training private pilots and ATC cadets on an Air Ministry contract basis, perhaps the most numerous being the light and dark blue machines operated by Air Schools Ltd at Wolverhampton, Derby and Elstree. When in 1956 the Air Registration Board (predecessors of today's Airworthiness Division of the Civil Aviation Authority) mistrusted aircraft with wooden box spars, most Magisters were scrapped, but a handful remained in private ownership for a few years. So, in effect, a good aeroplane died prematurely.

The Exhibit: P6382. One of only three preserved airworthy Magisters in the world. Often incorrectly quoted as being G-AJDR, as the aircraft arrived at Old Warden wearing that registration. However, logbook inspection revealed an earlier change of fuselage (to which an aeroplane's identify is attached) to that of P6382, which had not held a civil registration. Restored to fly by Shuttleworth apprentices, building-in components from three specimens.

At the Shuttleworth Pageant on 5 September 1993, P6382 was one of three Magisters in the air together for the first time in 37 years.

1941: HAWKER SEA HURRICANE 1b

Acquired 1961

Span: 40 ft
Empty weight: 4670 lb
Power: 1030 hp Rolls-Royce Merlin III 12-cylinder
liquid-cooled Vee

The Hawker Hurricane was the first of the British monoplane fighters, progressively replacing Gloster Gauntlets and Gladiators from December 1937, when No. 111 Squadron at Northolt became the first operational RAF unit to receive the new type. By the outbreak of World War II in 1939, eighteen RAF squadrons were equipped with Hurricanes, compared with nine that used Spitfires. This two-to-one ratio applied still during the Battle of Britain in the summer of 1940, in which Hurricanes shot down more enemy aircraft than all other defences — air and ground — combined.

Although the Hurricane went through a less visual development process than its partner, the Spitfire, there were many changes during the type's operational career. The traditional Hawker-style fuselage of fabric-covered tubular metal construction that had been used on the Hart, Fury and others before it remained throughout, but early in the production run the wings, originally with fabric covering, became stressed-skin metal covered. Initially the propeller was a large two-bladed wooden, fixed pitch type, but soon this gave way to a three-blade, two-pitch design and later a constant-speed unit was fitted. Each stage offered an improvement in performance. Power, too, was increased — by 250 hp with the introduction of the Hurricane II. However, perhaps it was in the roles for which the type was used and the equipment needed to achieve them that the most noticeable changes occurred. Early specimens had eight .303in. machine-guns, while Mark II Cs had four 20 mm guns and provision for externally-slung bombs beneath the wings and II Ds carried two large underwing 40 mm Vickers 'S' guns for tank-busting. This was a task in which they achieved outstanding success against Rommel's forces in the Western Desert and against the Japanese in Burma. Hurricanes were in action in every theatre of war.

The Sea Hurricane emerged in 1941; perhaps its most significant battle involvement in RN service was during Operation Pedestal, covering the Malta convoy in August 1942. Also a Naval Squadron operated Hurricanes in the Western Desert. Other nautical duties included serving with the Merchant Ship Fighter Unit, on convoy protection work, using aircraft fitted with catapult spools but not arrester hooks. There is some confusion over precise numbers of Sea Hurricane variants, but research reveals that about 680 were built or converted.

12,780 Hurricanes were built in Britain and a further 1451 in Canada. The last RAF squadron to use the type was No. 6, which operated Mark IVs in Palestine until January 1947. Today a Hurricane II serves with the Battle of Britain Memorial Flight and three others are in civil ownership.

The Exhibit: Built by Canadian Car & Foundry at Fort William, Ontario in the period December 1940 – January 1941 as a Hurricane 1. Taken on charge at 13MU (Henlow) on 18 March 1941 and then stored at 5MU (Kemble) until 27 June 1941 when it was issued to General Aircraft Ltd for conversion to Sea Hurricane 1b standard. Test flown on 16 July 1941. Delivered to Yeovilton (HMS *Heron*) 19 June 1941. Collected by No. 880 Sqn (then at St Merryn) on 29 July 1941. The squadron moved to RNAS Twatt in the Orkney Isles in August 1941 and then to Sumburgh, in the Shetlands, to work with 14 Group RAF. Z7015 left Sumburgh on 7 October 1941 bound for Macrihanish and HMS *Indomitable*, but when the Squadron embarked on 13-14 October, Z7015 was absent.

The next definite date is 10 February 1942 when Z7015 was flown from Hatston to Donibristle by Peter Hutton, a No. 801 Sqn pilot. On 5 April 1942 Z7015 was delivered to David Rosenfield Ltd., Barton, Manchester, for repair. It was 7 December 1942 before Z7015 left Barton for Ringway and then Yeovilton where it was issued to No. 759 Sqn and probably coded Y1-L. By the end of 1943 Z7015 had been delivered to Loughborough College for use as an instructional airframe in which capacity it served until 1961 when it was transferred to the Shuttleworth Collection.

After two false starts the restoration was formalised as a joint venture between the Imperial War Museum, Duxford and the Shuttleworth Collection, the work being carried out by the same team of volunteers who restored the Collection's Spitfire Vc AR501.

1941: SUPERMARINE SPITFIRE Vc

Acquired 1961

Span: 32 ft 2 in
Empty weight: 5200 lb
Power: 1440 hp Rolls-Royce Merlin 45 or 46, 12-cylinder
liquid-cooled Vee

Perhaps no aircraft is as well known to so many people as is the Spitfire. For many years almost a legend, the true Supermarine Spitfire first saw daylight under its wheels on 5 March 1936, although the type owed much to the earlier S.6 seaplanes of Schneider Trophy fame. Before the familiar elliptical wing of the Spitfire appeared, however, a single-seat fighter designated the Supermarine F7/30 had flown, with an inverted gull (cranked) wing, a fixed undercarriage, an open cockpit and powered by the steam-cooled Rolls-Royce Goshawk engine. Strangely, this fulfilled the requirements of the original Air Ministry specification, but its famous designer, the late R J Mitchell, was at work on something better on a private venture basis.

So the Spitfire was born. Conforming to a revised A.M. requirement F37/34, this incorporated the new 1030 hp Merlin engine and (apart from a few very early examples) eight instead of four machine-guns in the wings. Within three months of the prototype's first flight, an initial order was placed for 310 aircraft, but production difficulties delayed deliveries and the first batch was five months late in reaching Service units. However, such was the Spitfire's success that shortly after the start of World War II orders totalled 4000 aircraft.

The first Spitfires were delivered to No. 19 Squadron at Duxford, arriving in July 1938, eight months later than the first Hawker Hurricanes joined No. 111 Squadron at Northolt; in each case these new aircraft were replacements for ageing Gloster Gauntlets, which were the Gladiator's immediate predecessor. The early Spitfires had two-blade fixed-pitch propellers and relatively poor take-off performance, but the type was ripe for development, with three-blade variable-pitch propellers and domed cockpit canopies becoming standard equipment while the aircraft was still at the Mark I stage.

By the outbreak of war nine RAF Squadrons were equipped with Spitfires, with eighteen squadrons using Hurricanes. The two types shared the brunt of the Battle of Britain between them, with the Spitfire's superior speed and the Hurricane's manoeuvrability used to maximum advantage.

Development and mark numbers followed in rapid succession. From August 1940, IIbs exchanged the Mark I's standard eight-gun layout for four .303in. machine-guns and two 20 mm cannon. Although best known for its activities as a fighter, early in the Spitfire's career it was adapted for high-speed high-level photographic reconnaissance, stripped of all armament, with production of the PR IV amounting to 230 aircraft.

Some marks were more notable than others and, without doubt, the V was a winner. With the Merlin 45 developing 410 hp more than the early variant, both the performance and the extent of the aircraft's use were increased. Mark Vs were the first to be used as fighter bombers, taking part in offensive sweeps across Europe, and were the first to be used extensively overseas. Many operated with clipped wings for increased performance and roll-rate at low level. The V was followed by the IX and these two variants became the most widely used of all marks.

Throughout the Spitfire's operational life, development continued. Some were fitted with extended wings of forty-foot span to improve high-altitude performance to combat high-flying German raiders; the rear top fuselage was lowered to provide improved all-round view from a bubble canopy, the rudder was extended upwards to a pointed tip and a four-bladed propeller was introduced. After the IX, however, the type underwent some of its most drastic modifications, exchanging the Merlin for the Griffon and offering a marked change in appearance with a longer nose and larger-chord rudder. One of the most impressive performers among the late-mark Spitfires was the PR 19, which outclassed the early jet fighters at altitude; it was this variant that carried out the last operational sortie by any front-line Spitfire, with a reconnaissance by a machine of No. 81 Squadron over Malaya on 1 April 1954.

At one time in the late fifties, only a single Spitfire (Mark Vc AB 510/G-AISU, owned by its makers) was flying, but progressively the number has increased. The Royal Air Force Battle of Britain Flight at Coningsby in Lincolnshire operates a Mark II, a Vb and three 19s, while privately-owned machines include a I, a rare two-seat Mark T VIII, a pair of IXs, and a Griffon-powered XIV. More are being rebuilt.

The Exhibit: Mark Vc AR501/G-ASII. Built by Westland Aircraft at Yeovil, Somerset, and issued to No. 310 (Czech) Squadron at Duxford in 1942. Research in 1992 revealed that AR501 flew several sorties in 1942/43 escorting United States 8th Army Air Force B-24s and B-17s, including the famous *Memphis Belle* of 91st Bombardment Group. Later taken on the strength of the RAF's Central Gunnery School. Used post-war as an instructional airframe at Loughborough College, before transfer to the Collection and restoration to flying condition for use in the film *The Battle of Britain*. Stored for several years at Old Warden; later restoration to a very high standard was completed by a volunteer crew at Duxford. The only Spitfire flying with an original DH three-blade bracket propeller.

On 30 October 1990 sent to Westlands for 50-year-check on a non-destructive testing survey and to be totally wax-injected internally. Returned with a clean bill of health.

1946: DHC-I CHIPMUNK   Acquired 1969

Span: 34 ft 4 in
Empty weight: 1417 lb
Power: 145 hp DH Gipsy Major 8 (10/2 in civil use)
    4-cylinder inverted inline

The Chipmunk was a logical development in the long line of de Havilland light aeroplanes, although it was unusual in two ways: firstly, wooden construction had given way to an all-metal structure and secondly, it was designed and originally produced in Canada, which accounts for the DHC designation.

The prototype Chipmunk, CF-DIO-X, flew for the first time at Toronto on 22 May 1946 and 218 were built in Canada, with a gap of more than five years between the two main production batches; the last sixty for the Royal Canadian Air Force emerged as late as 1956. In Britain, production started in 1949 to Air Ministry specification 8/48, with first deliveries to Oxford University Air Squadron at Kidlington (now Oxford Airport) in February 1950. Subsequently the type equipped all 17 UASs, the Reserve Flying Schools, the Primary Flying Squadron and, later, the Air Experience Flights that provide flying for ATC and CCF cadets.

The Chipmunk was relatively expensive as a new aeroplane, so home civil sales from the factory were restricted to a pair for the Ministry of Transport and Civil Aviation and six for Air Service Training at Hamble. However, the RAF Reserve schools closed in 1953 and after a period in storage at Maintenance Units, large numbers were sold. They were nearly-new aircraft and inexpensive to buy, so they appealed to several flying schools and clubs, but the airworthiness authority of the time deemed the Service version, the T.10, to fall short of civil requirements and called for extensive and expensive modifications. The result was a civil variant designated the T.22. The largest numbers of these were operated by the Airways Aero Club (replacing Auster Aiglets) and by Air Schools Ltd, the latter's light and dark blue machines replacing ageing Magisters (Hawk Trainer IIIs) in 1956-57.

The Chipmunk was one of the most pleasant light aeroplanes to handle, with well harmonized controls that were more akin to those of a heavier machine. However, as with most trainers, it suffered from spin recovery problems; these resulted first in the fitting of broad-chord rudders, which achieved little result, followed several years later by fuselage strakes.

The DHC-1 is a far more significant aeroplane than most people appear to appreciate. It has outstripped both the legendary Avro 504 and the Tiger Moth in terms of length of military service, with the unique distinction that after more than forty years with the RAF, it served until 1993 with all three British Services: in the Royal Air Force with the Air Experience Flights and in 1979 reintroduced as the primary trainer; at Middle Wallop where all army pilots receive their basic tuition on the type; and with the Britannia Flight at Plymouth to give air experience to cadets from the Royal Naval College at Dartmouth. Roughly comparable numbers are in civil use with groups and private owners, although Service numbers have been reduced from 1993 as RN and RAF elementary flying training is contracted to civilian companies using Slingsby T-67 Fireflies.

The Exhibit: WB 588/G-AOTD. Constructor's No. 0040. Built 1950. An early release from the RAF following closure of the Reserve Schools. Stored at RAE Farnborough and later Bedford before being given to the Collection. Stored again for ten years until restoration was undertaken by a volunteer group from British Aerospace, Kingston.

First flew in Shuttleworth ownership in August 1983. Subsequently repainted in Oxford University Air Squadron markings.

4
Other Aviation Exhibits

Although the Shuttleworth Collection is known mainly for its famous historic aeroplanes and for the fact that they fly, the hangars at Old Warden serve as homes for many other items of note. These include aero-engines, propellers, instruments, models, flying clothing and, of course, some very early veteran cars, with which the Collection was started as long ago as 1928.

Although many people think that the aeroplanes form the key features in the Collection, largely because many of them are sole survivors of their types, we must not overlook the significance of the many road vehicles on display. Although few in number when compared with the aircraft, there are some early cars with considerable claims to historic merit. Their details were omitted from the previous guide, known as *Shuttleworth: the Historic Aeroplanes*, but this new book is more comprehensive in its coverage and the title has been changed to reflect that growth.

Below: There is a complete range of Rolls-Royce aero-engines on view in the Collection.

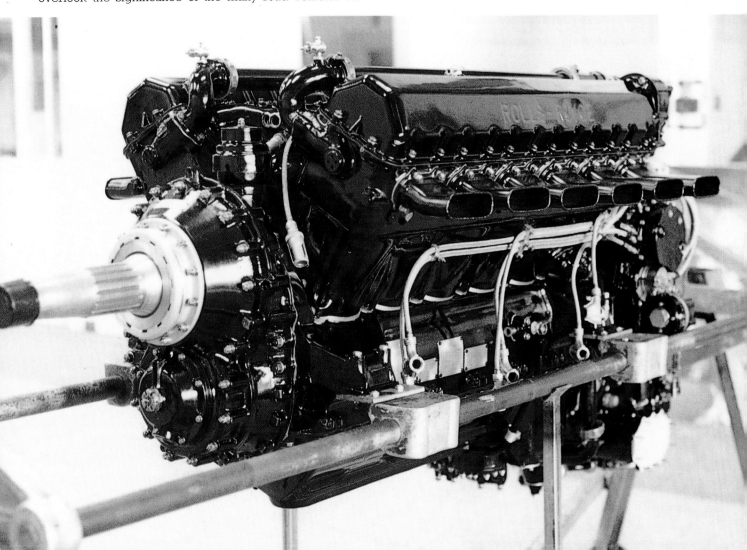

Aircraft equipment

Engines

Perhaps the most conspicuous range of aircraft-related items on display around the hangars is the comprehensive selection of aero-engines. In the early days of flight, the pioneers were severely restricted because of the lack of suitable motive power, so they learnt to design, build and fly gliders, with people such as Otto Lilienthal and the Scotsman Percy Pilcher achieving considerable success in the 1890s. Although serious thought was given to the possible use of steam power, no practical progress was made until the petrol engine became a workable proposition, for although a Benz internal combustion engine was working on the road in a three-wheeled motor-carriage as far back as 1885, much more development was needed before this new power source would be capable of lifting man into the air. Certainly balloons had flown under power in earlier years, but this happened with an *aeroplane* in December 1903 when the Wright brothers achieved the first powered, controlled flight.

In the Collection at Old Warden the aircraft engines range from some of the very earliest units to the end of the piston era. Also, to complete the picture of basic development, some early jet engines are on display. However perhaps the most unusual really practical aero-engine of earlier times is the rotary, on which the crankshaft remains stationary with the crankcase and cylinders revolving around it. Power is controlled by careful use of separate levers for the supply of fuel and air to create the required mixture for smooth running. A partly-sectioned example, in the form of a 110 hp Clerget of 1915 as used in several World War I aircraft, can be put into motion (electrically powered) at the touch of a switch by a visitor.

The pressure of war in the 1914-18 period produced some rapid development in aero-engines, in terms of both power output and reliability. Whereas in 1912 the 50 hp Gnome rotary had been near the top of the available performance range, by 1916 Rolls-Royce had produced the Falcon twelve-cylinder liquid-cooled Vee that produced 275 hp. Attached to the famous Bristol F.2B Fighter, the combination resulted in perhaps the most effective fighting aeroplane of the time. The Falcon is of special significance in the presentation of history of the aero-engine, for it was the start of a long line of twelve-cylinder Vees from the Rolls-Royce stable; these included the Kestrel (to be seen in action in the Collection's Hawker Hind of 1935), the Merlin (in the Collection's Hawker Hurricane and Supermarine Spitfire) and the Griffon, the last, largest and most powerful of the line which remained in Service use until 1992 when the RAF's last Squadron (No. 8) of Avro Shackletons was re-equipped with Boeing Sentries. The Collection includes a comprehensive display of Rolls-Royce piston engines.

There were many other producers of power plants for aircraft use and some of these followed entirely different design concepts. Armstrong-Siddeley and Bristol centred their production on static (as opposed to the earlier rotary) radials; these relied on airflow for cooling. The former company produced a wide band of different engines, many of which were built in relatively small numbers and which differed in detail despite carrying their original names: the Collection has three specimens of the Genet radial, which can have either five or seven cylinders! A Genet provides the power for the diminutive Southern Martlet single-seat biplane of 1929; a slightly larger Mongoose is in the Hawker Tomtit trainer and the Lynx in the Avro Tutor is heavier and more powerful again. The ubiquitous Avro Anson worked its way through several marks of Cheetah engines.

Bristol radials were mounted on numerous military and civil types and, after active wartime careers in such machines as the Bristol Blenheim, Beaufort and Beaufighter, Short Stirling, Handley Page Hampden and Halifax and Vickers-Armstrongs Wellington, these continued into the post-war era on the Vickers Viking, Bristol Freighter, Handley Page Hermes and others that formed mainstays of the commercial air transport sector before the 'propjet' and the pure jet took over.

One name in the field of aircraft design and production — de Havilland — played an equally significant role in providing power for Britain's lighter aeroplanes. The Gipsy range, which extended from four to six to twelve cylinders, could be found on an almost limitless number of types from the early thirties onwards. Nearly all Moths, including the de Havilland Tiger Moth of World War II training fame, were propelled into the air by four-cylinder Gipsies, while the six-cylinder Gipsy appeared in the DH Dragon-Rapide domestic airliner and the world-famous DH 88 Comet that won the MacRobertson Air Race from England to Australia in 1934. The Gipsy Twelve powered the DH Albatross four-engined airliner and one of the world's only surviving examples of this engine is held by the Collection.

These, of course, are the famous names, but as with aeroplanes, many other companies entered the field of design and production of engines that fulfilled significant roles. Names such as ABC, Anzani, Airdisco, Alvis, J A Prestwick (JAP), Pobjoy, Blackburn (more widely known for aeroplanes than for their power units, although many of these were used), and others between them produced engines for all possible purposes. Many of these are on show at Old Warden, while some of the more notable types can be seen on board the aeroplanes in the Collection, with second specimens available for closer inspection in the static exhibition.

Propellers

Although each piston engine is designed to generate a specific power output, all this energy is of no value unless it can be transmitted effectively. In the case of the road vehicle, this is relatively straightforward and predictable, with the power being directed, usually via a gearbox, to the wheels. With an aeroplane there can be no such direct contact and we must rely on the efficiency of the propeller to produce the required amount of thrust. An engine installed in one type of aeroplane may require a propeller with different characteristics from that in another machine with an identical power output. Diameter, pitch and blade width are among the variables that must be calculated accurately if an aeroplane is to perform at its best. In many instances, aircraft have been tested with a series of different propellers with an equally variable number of performance achievements. In the simplest terms, a propeller with blades set at 'fine' pitch (which will produce high revolutions) will provide good results on take-off and climb, but on the cruise in level flight it will be inefficient, especially in terms of fuel consumption. At the other end of the design scale, coarse-pitch blades will give good cruise performance, but the initial 'get-up-and-go' quality may be almost totally absent. So all early propellers were designed to a compromise that gave acceptable, if not sparkling, performances throughout the operating range.

By the 1930s two-pitch propellers had been made to work. The principle here equates to a car with two gears, but using 'fine' for take-off and 'coarse' for normal flight. Some aircraft, though, enjoyed progressive performance improvements as the propellers were updated, even though the engine power remained constant: perhaps the Hawker Hurricane was one of the most notable among these. The earliest production aircraft were fitted with large two-blade fixed-pitch propellers, which later were replaced by three-blade two-pitch units and finally these gave way to variable-pitch constant-speed airscrews — to use a term of the time. In this last type, the pitch of the propeller was under the full control of the pilot, who used a lever alongside the throttle lever and the desired power setting was achieved by balancing the correct boost and rpm. Also, when changes were made to the boost setting or to the airspeed, e.g. in a dive, the revs remained constant. The Hurricane gained more than 20 mph in level flight speed, together with a substantially improved rate of climb and a better performance at height.

Some of the propellers on display are among the earliest designs and it is possible to study the development of these items through to the later types of constant-speed variable-pitch propeller such as the one fitted to the Collection's Supermarine Spitfire Vc. Remember, when looking at these, that the propeller is perhaps the most critical single piece of equipment that determines an aeroplane's standards of performance.

Instruments

Early aeroplanes had few of these. The Collection's 1912 Blackburn, for example, is fitted with an rpm gauge as the only dial in the cockpit. This is because the rotary engine — as already described — was especially sensitive to settings of the air and petrol levers in order to attain optimum performance and this needed (and today still needs) to be checked visually. As time went on, though, more instruments appeared and not long passed before the air-speed indicator and altimeter (although initially a very crude and difficult-to-read device) were placed on the panel, to be joined by the oil pressure gauge, which many of us even today consider to provide the most important information that a pilot needs for sustained flight. Interestingly, airspeed information was provided on some machines by a spring-loaded pointer (activated by forward speed) to a graduated metal strip mounted on an outboard wing strut; this early device can be seen on several of the aeroplanes in the Collection. Alas, I have not found a case in which the cockpit dial and the strut gauge offer similar answers!

Cabins of many modern aeroplanes (light aircraft included) have panels that provide the required flight information in forms that are strange to the traditional mind, but here we are concerned with development up to, but not beyond, World War II. By this time a form of cockpit commonality was available through use of the 'standard panel', which was fitted to all British aeroplanes except elementary trainers. This offered a considerable bonus to a pilot when transferring from one aircraft type to another, for the six basic flight instruments (airspeed indicator, altimeter, vertical speed indicator, turn and slip indicator, directional gyro and artificial horizon) were to be found in identical positions on all types.

Not all the exhibits are always on view. Here the Blackburn undergoes essential restoration in a workshop.

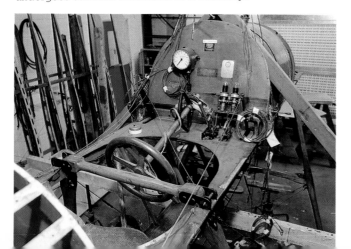

Flying clothing

Early pilots needed to wear much more in the way of warm clothing than is the case today. Fur-lined flying boots were a necessity and not just a luxury when climbing to operational height early on a frosty February morning. Two pairs of gloves — silk inners and leather outers — enabled the fingers to retain some feel for at least the first part of a flight. Helmets, too, were essential, initially with no communication facility, then with attachments for the earpieces for Gosport speaking tubes, and finally having connections and fittings for use with radio and electrical intercom.

Items of uniform are exhibited, including those used by the Royal Flying Corps in the 1914-18 war.

Other aviation items

Lighter-than-air

Various items relating to the first era of airships are in this section: key exhibits are scale models of two famous airships — the R100 and the R101. The first of these was built as a result of an Air Ministry contract for the construction by private enterprise of an airship for commercial transportation purposes. The second, the R101, was to be built by the Air Ministry as a Government venture. In each case the specification called for an empty weight of not more than ninety tons and a lifting capacity of 150 tons, therefore assuring a usable lift of sixty tons. Eating and sleeping accommodation for 100 passengers was to be provided and the required performance was to include a maximum speed of not less than 70 mph.

The R100 was designed by Barnes Wallis, whose fame extended into many later spheres, including design of the geodetic structure on the Vickers Wellington and the concept of the bouncing bomb used for dam-busting. This airship was built at Howden in Yorkshire and, powered by six 700 hp Rolls-Royce Condor engines, took to the air for the first time on 16 December 1929. After many months of trials, with numerous modifications and improvements, the R100 flew from Cardington (only four miles from Old Warden) to Montreal on a flight lasting seventy-eight hours. The journey home was completed in more favourable conditions in fifty-seven-and-a-half hours.

The R101 was built at Cardington and, as with its private enterprise counterpart, required many early modifications following its first flight, which was on 14 October 1929. It had five Beardmore engines, each of 585 hp, but one of these was used solely in the take-off and landing phases as power for enabling the ship to move astern. Unfortunately, the 101's performance fell far short of the required lift figure and the middle bay was extended to provide space for an extra gas-bag. After only one trial flight in this revised structural configuration, the

Above: A sectioned rotary engine in the main works hangar.

airship was launched from Cardington on an intended flight to India, but near Beauvais in France it failed and crashed. As a result, the R100 was withdrawn from service and sold for scrap.

The earliest airships were virtually balloons or gas-filled envelopes, with the engines and accommodation suspended by rigging. Later, as hanging weight increased, rigid keels were fitted to the base of the envelope to support the load and this became known as the semi-rigid type. Eventually, further structural stiffening became necessary and a full framework was used, leading to the category of rigid airship. Both the R100 and the R101 were of this more advanced type.

There are several other exhibits related to lighter-than-air flight and among these is the 30 hp JAP eight-cylinder Vee engine used on the small airship *City of Cardiff*, which allegedly was the first powered flying-machine of any kind to fly on the west side of the British Isles.

Models

In addition to the airships, there are models of many aeroplanes, including an accurate scale reproduction of the original Wright Flier of 1903. Smaller models of other historic aircraft are exhibited on a rotational basis.

5

The Historic Vehicles

As the Collection started in 1928 when Richard Shuttleworth acquired his first veteran car, the road vehicles deserve a greater level of attention than they have received. The previous edition of the guide concentrated mainly on the aviation exhibits and this new chapter sets out to fill that gap in the Shuttleworth story.

Richard had a strong interest in cars and he had the unusual fortune (for that time) to be in a family that owned several. His mother had a 5 hp Wolseley in about 1905 and his father was a regular early motorist. Later Richard became an active racing driver.

First among the acquisitions was the Panhard Levassor, which is believed to have been built in 1900, but the precise date of its origin is obscure and in its earliest days it underwent a number of technical modifications. Believed to have been used by King Edward VII to attend Ascot races in 1901, Lord Rothschild's chauffeur is alleged to have sold it to Richard Shuttleworth for twenty-five shillings – or £1.25p in today's currency. Details of this and the other vehicles in the wide range housed at Old Warden follow . . .

INTERNATIONAL BENZ 1898 (T.274)

3½ hp; 1045 cc; single cylinder; belt-driven; 3 speed – no reverse.

Two-seater dog cart. went into commercial production. Price £320. Took part in the Brighton Run; it did not finish in 1932, but completed the run in 1934 and 1936.

MORS 1899 Model A Petit Duc (F 7)

4 hp; 2 cylinders; horizontally opposed.

The original ignition system, peculiar to Mors, has been

1901 Locomobile Steam Car

replaced by a H.T. Magneto. Originally the spark was obtained by breaking the circuit of a low tension current produced by a dynamo drawn by the engine. This car was the first private car registered in Essex on 1 January 1904 and given F 7 – the first six numbers being reserved for official cars. Its first owner was the Rev R V D Graves, Vicar of Tolleshunt D'Arcy, Essex, who paid about £200 for it.

DAIMLER 1899 (SC 8778)

6 hp. Unrestored.

Wagonette type body. No details of how acquired. Stated to have been in use until 1924. 2 cylinder water-cooled engine of 1525 cc. Tiller steering.

PANHARD LEVASSOR 1900 (TM 19)

12 hp; 4 cylinder water-cooled; 4-speed gearbox. Body by Morgan & Co.

Firm originally machinery manufacturers, but undertook making Daimler engines in France, then progressed to complete vehicles of their own design using Daimler engines, achieving notable success with one of their cars in the Paris-Bordeaux-Paris race of June 1895. Originally this vehicle was owned by Lord Rothschild; King Edward VII was driven in it to Ascot Races in 1901. The present body dates from that year.
Completed the first Brighton Run in 1928 and numerous times since.

MAROT-GARDON 1900 (DPC 489)

Uses a 2½ hp De Dion engine.

Capable of conversion into a single-seat tricycle. Top speed about 20 mph. Similar machines were produced by De Dion, Singer Cycle Co of Coventry and the Riley Lycee Co, also of Coventry.

ARROL JOHNSTON 1901 HX4110, Maker's Serial No 76 (SN 35)

12 hp; 2 cylinder; water-cooled; 4 gears; 6-seater. This firm started as the Mo Car Syndicate of Paisley and became Arrol Johnston Motor Car Co in 1905. The engine is carried at the rear and has two water-cooled cylinders each containing two pistons. These work via rocking levers to a single crankshaft through connecting rods. Cooling is by water circulated by a pump; an injector is fitted to enable the water tank to be filled by drawing from ponds, rivers etc. Purchased from Arrol Johnston Ltd (in liquidation) in October 1931 and driven to Old Warden 19 December. In 1933 Brighton Run it averaged 9.8 mph.

LOCOMOBILE 1901 (FM 63)

A typical light American steamer. 5½ hp steam engine; 2 cylinders, bore 2½", stroke 3½". Fuel: petrol. Vertical multi-tube boiler. Final drive by chain. Took about 12 minutes to raise steam from cold. Price about £200. Has taken part successfully in the Brighton Run.

BABY PEUGEOT 1902 (AA1417)

5 hp; single cylinder; water-cooled.

Peugeot Frères originally were manufacturing iron-mongers, then switched to cycle making and progressed to motor cars. One of the brothers, Armand was trained in England. This vehicle was used in large numbers in the early years of this century. Price £195. Has competed successfully in some 16 Brighton runs since 1929.

DE DIETRICH 1903 (A1853)

24 hp; 4-cylinder engine; 4-speed gearbox & reverse. Firm originally railway equipment builders; engaged Eltone Bugatti as a consultant in 1902. First owned by Sir George McKenzie of Tempsford Park, Bedfordshire, the De Dietrich was originally fitted with a Tonnau type body, then in 1905 converted to a Shooting body with a detachable hood. The present racing body was fitted by Richard Shuttleworth to whom the car was registered 5 November 1928. Regularly driven in the Brighton Run. Achieved 60 mph at Brooklands.

1902 Baby Peugeot

1903 De Dietrich

1900 Panhard Levassor

RICHARD BRAZIER 1903 (H 127)

24 hp; 4 cylinder; water-cooled, 6-seater. Firm was French. Georges Richard was a pioneer car maker and M. Brazier was originally a designer for the Mors Concern. Pre 1914, the majority of London taxis were produced by this firm, under the name of Unic. First registered in Dorset on 11 December 1903; owned by Lt-Col M F Gage and later sold to a Captain J V Taylor who ran it until 1914. It was presented to Richard Shuttleworth by a relation of Captain Taylor who served in the same regiment as Richard. Restoration commenced in 1956.

WOLSELEY 1912 (BM 2181)

24/30 hp; Limousine; type M5. Ordered by Col F Shuttleworth 22 February 1912. Chassis laid down 23 May, delivered 17 July 1912. Invoice price £803.15s.10d. Used by the family until the 1920s. Restored in the late 1980s. The total mileage is believed to be less than 2500.

CROSSLEY 1912 Model T.5 (Y.1616)

15 hp; 4 cylinder; chassis no. 1628.

Smaller version of the 20/25 hp used by the RFC as a Staff car, with a light tender version. First ordered in 1912, with a trial batch of six. By 1918 some 10,000 were in use. This vehicle purchased in 1956 from a Mr Pyddoke of Sevenoaks, Kent. It is stated to be in largely original conditions.

MORRIS OXFORD 1913 (No registration)

10 hp; 4-cylinder water-cooled.

William Morris, later to become Lord Nuffield, had originally been engaged in the cycle world and made his first car in 1912. He set out to bring motoring within reach of the ordinary man and this he achieved in no small way. This type made its first appearance at the 1913 Manchester Show and made a most favourable impression. The Shuttleworth example has a White and Poppe engine, as did other early Morris cars and was delivered to the Haslemere Motor Co on 23 March 1914. Price was £180.

HUCKS 1918 (?) (MP 8433)

Developed towards the end of the First World War by Captain B C Hucks, a pioneer pre-war pilot and chief test pilot of the Aircraft Manufacturing Co. As aero-engines were becoming increasingly powerful the customary method of starting by swinging the propeller by hand posed a problem, in some cases causing accidents to mechanics. Hucks then devised, in the days before such built-in starting methods as gas, inertia, cartridge and electrical were introduced, a mechanical starter using as a base a Ford Model T chassis to which was fitted an overhead shaft powered from the vehicle's engine. The shaft was adjustable for height and a claw to connect with a dog on the aircraft propeller; the shaft was able to move telescopically against a spring loading. To start an engine the starter is driven up to the aeroplane and a ground crew member adjusts the alignment and engages the claw and dog; then the driver reverses a short distance to put the claw under tension load, after which he disengages the engine from the transmission, engaging the drive to the shaft. On getting the starting signal from the pilot, he applies the engine after which the aeroplane engine usually starts after one or two revolutions. This releases the claw from the propeller, drawn back by the spring mechanism, the drive to the overhead shaft is then disengaged and the starter is reversed away from the aeroplane. In 1920, its use was made mandatory for starting all military aero-engines, except for the 100 hp Monosoupape.

Manufacture of the Starter was by the Aircraft Manufacturing Co, forerunners of the de Havilland Co, where apprentices restored this example in the 1950s.

JOWETT 1926 (NM 8092)

Light Four Type C C/N 66386. Used by Richard Shuttleworth as a runabout and utility car. Under restoration. Engine 7 hp, water-cooled, horizontally-opposed 2-cylinder. Bodywork panelled in aluminium.

AUSTIN BURNHAM 1931 (GT 1944)

12 hp: 4 cylinder saloon deluxe.

Cost new £288 + £3.10s. (£3.50p) delivery charge. This car is still in its original paintwork, was unused for many years, with only one owner. Received as a bequest from Mr A W T Vale of Streatham, London, who use it from new to 1956 and was stored in his garage until received at Old Warden in 1989. It is owned by the Shuttleworth Veteran Aeroplane Society.

AUSTIN 7 (AGG 163) Type AAK Open Tourer – first introduced 1934

Car No AAK 903; engine no. M 217852

This car differs in some points from the standard production model, tyre sizes 400 + 17 in lieu of 350 + 19, the larger ones for the 1935 model. Chrome lamps also for 1935. The bumpers seem to be a later addition.

RAILTON 1937 (JNM 700)

2-seater coupe; 8-cylinder engine; 4168 cc capacity.

Purchased by Richard Shuttleworth in the late 1930s; he

had joined the Board of Railton Cars in 1933. He began to built it up as an open sports car in 1939, but after his death the work was completed by Blanchflowers of Kettering for Mrs Shuttleworth who sold it in 1952. It passed through several hands until 1976 when purchased by Princess Charlotte, a relative of Richard Shuttleworth, who placed it in her husband's auto museum at Schloss Langenburg.

BICYCLES

1819 Ladies Hobby Horse. On loan from Science Museum. Believed made by Denis Johnson who patented this machine in 1818 and made a large number in 1819. This example believed to have been purchased by the Duke of Malborough of the time.

1860 Treadle drive boneshaker.

1868 Boneshaker. Constructed with iron frame and wooden wheels. The brake is operated by twisting the handlebars, working on rear wheel only.

1877 Starley 2-seat quadricycle. Can be converted to a single seater by altering the frame.

1879 Penny Farthing or Ordinary (2 examples)

1901 Albone 'Ivel' ladies cycle. Made by D Albone, a well known pioneer cyclist, in his works in Biggleswade

1944 BSA paratroop cycle. Foldable. Introduced to increase mobility of airborne troops

1962 Moulton. The designer of this cycle had always been a keen cyclist and had also studied rubber suspension systems. Since the basic design of cycles had remained unchanged for some 70 years, he decided to improve upon the design and produced a cycle incorporating small wheels, a new frame and rubber suspension, thereby giving a more comfortable ride. The machine folds up easily to fit into a car boot.

HORSEDRAWN VEHICLES

Barouche 1870. Used as a town carriage; this example, drawn by two horses, was used at the weddings of Richard Shuttleworth's parents and grandparents

Brougham Introduced by Lord Brougham in about 1840, as an economical type of carriage suitable for town use; it is drawn by one horse

Governess Cart c.1907. Used mainly in the country for conveyance of children and elderly people, it seats about 4 people who sit with their backs to the wheels & facing each other. Usually drawn by a pony.

Omnibus 1880/90. Used by the Shuttleworth family, usually to convey guests and their baggage to and from the local railway stations.

American buggy The design originated in America. This example was driven by Col Shuttleworth with a fast pony.

Dog cart c.1904. Used in the country for carrying gun dogs and their owners to shoots, or for general haulage purposes

Rickshaw A manually-propelled passenger vehicle, widely used as a taxi in the Far East, sometimes hauled by a person on a bicycle

Phaeton A type of bath chair which dates from late Victorian times

FIRE ENGINES

2 manual fire engines are on display
    1844 ex-Hitchin. Based on Newshams patents of 1721 & 1728. On loan from Hitchin museum.
    1790 Read's engine.
    Both these engines, operated by teams of men, are mainly constructed of wood, with metal pumps and leather seals. The hoses are of leather. Both engines have cisterns of small capacity, which would have needed to be kept topped up by a bucket brigade. The larger engine would have had an output of about 80 gallons a minute.

MOTORCYCLES

1900 Singer Motor Wheel. Driven by a Compact motor of 2 hp, 211 cc. Made by Perks & Birch of Coventry, with the complete power unit contained within the wheel. Air-cooling is assisted by the wheel spokes. Ignition by magneto. The carburettor is combined with the fuel tank holding ½ gallon of petrol, which is sufficient for 50 miles. Top speed 25 mph. Pedals can be used to assist, if needs be in going up hills. It was claimed however that gradients of 1 in 6 could be climbed without pedal assistance.

Aurora 1904 2¼ hp

Scott Combination 1919

Triumph SD 1923 550 cc 3-speed gearbox, 4 hp

Raleigh Type 14 1927 250 cc

Ariel 1929 550 cc Side valve (Loaned by A Preslent)

BSA WD Type 1937

Rudge 1938 500 cc (Loaned by A Brett)

Norton RAC Combinartion. The last one to have been used by RAC patrols.

6
Maintaining airworthiness

By Chris Morris,
Chief Engineer of the Shuttleworth Collection

Chris Morris served his apprenticeship with de Havilland at Hatfield, rebuilt several Tiger Moths whilst with Bowker Air Services and joined the Collection's engineering staff in 1979. He is now the Chief Engineer.

All the aircraft on display at the Collection need to withstand the scrutiny of the critical general public, day in and day out, for fifty-one weeks of the year. This task is repeated in museums around the country, with varying degrees of success; but this is no museum. It is a collection of fully functional aircraft. Not only that, but the engineering under the fabric and cowlings is far more instructional and fascinating than the exterior, and carries a higher responsibility for the Collection staff, because the aircraft are in a truly airworthy condition. Another element to be adhered to is that, within the bounds of airworthiness, the constructional methods and components must be as close as possible to the original, to satisfy the requirements of the Collection's educational status, and to ensure the historical

accuracy of the exhibit. The first criterion is relatively easy to adhere to; in fact, care has to be taken not to over embellish, with copper and aluminium not unnecessarily polished, various small items not obtrusively chromed or nickel plated, paint and varnished areas not too shiny. These items would readily attract the public's eye, but would not be historically correct as the manufacturers would not have released them from the factory like that. The second and third elements are often interlinked and contradictory, and safe and reliable alternatives must be sought. Obviously, the engineers would not try to use bamboo longerons, or cover the fabric in flour sizing, as was done in 1909 and before. At any one time, the Shuttleworth Collection maintains about thirty of its own aircraft in full airworthy condition and carries out some servicing of two or three loaned machines. All these are maintained by three full-time engineers, and one part-time and their workload is shared over six loose groups.

1. Major rebuilding, i.e. taking an aircraft out of store and completely stripping for a total refurbish.

This often means replacing most of the woodwork, either because of wood deterioration, or because the structural joints were glued using a casein type, which nowadays is not considered permanent. The metalwork often suffers badly, because when the aircraft was stored, for whatever reason, no preservative was applied. Also, when a metal bracket is clamped to wood, the slight moisture and acidity in the wood readily attacks the fitting. More often than not, parts of the airframe, engine, controls, instruments or other major items have gone missing down the way, and with a one-off aircraft as most tend to be, there is often no other reference, or written or drawn data. Reverse engineering is often the case, where a part is devised to meet the empty space, then designed, drawn, made and fitted. The Collection has been involved with major rebuilds on the Parnall Elf, Tiger Moth, Magister, LVG, Hawker Hind, and to a lesser extent the Comet. The current aircraft in rebuild is the Southern Martlet, a small single-seat biplane powered by a five-cylinder Genet, circa 1929. This aircraft will take several years to complete, as the majority of the work takes place in the winter, between other tasks.

Left: Refurbishment of the Bristol Boxkite's tail unit.
Right: Getting at the 'works' of the Avro 504K.

HAWKER HIND

1935

HIND ENGINE REMOVED
FOR COMPLETE O/HAUL

2. Refurbishing a current aircraft, for new fabric, plywood skinning, major inspections etc. or as a result of a mishap.

The unsupported fabric on the aircraft is an unbleached Irish linen, which seems to last twenty-five years or so if it is painted, or half that if it is doped clear, where the ultraviolet rays can pass readily through the clear dope, and rot the fabric. One such aircraft comes through the workshops about every two years or so, be it the Blackburn Monoplane, Deperdussin, Sopwith Pup, Hawker Tomtit, Avro 504, or Bristol Fighter, etc. The ply-covered aircraft last much longer, but ply replacements have been carried out on the Magister and Hermes Moth.

3. Deferred items held over to winter: items that can safely be rectified or inspected when a longer period of time is required and available.

This work takes a fair portion of the period between the last flying day at the end of the season, and hopefully preparing the aircraft in readiness for the first flying day in the spring. Such items could be a variable pitch propeller inspection, bench servicing of starters, generators, magnetos, voltage regulators and instruments, overhaul of worn pins, fittings and bushes in control circuits or undercarriages, adjustment of glands and seals in undercarriage items, repair of cracked exhausts, cowlings, replacement of tyres, bungees etc. At the beginning of the winter period, many of the aircraft are 'laid up', i.e. inhibited, or protected against condensation. Several engine tasks normally crop up, and are dealt with then.

4. Permit Renewals.

An airworthy aircraft must satisfy certain airworthiness criteria, as laid down and monitored by the Civil Aviation Authority, and executed or verified by licensed engineers. The aircraft are inspected for their Permits annually, and with thirty Permits, this works out at about four per month during the flying season. Ideally, with forward planning, the only work involved is minor inspection, and paperwork — as all the larger tasks should have been dealt with the previous winter.

5. Minor rectification or adjustment during the season.

These are normally snags, and if they can be safely deferred, invariably they are. However, if the aircraft has come into the workshops for an investigation, it is usually more cost effective to rectify the problem there and then. It is very rare for such aircraft, or any aircraft to miss the next flying display.

Previous page left: The famous DH 88 Comet undergoing engine tests before its first flight following rebuild.

Previous page right: The Hind awaiting its rebuilt engine.

6. Outside Work

If no major rebuilds or repairs are likely to come through the workshops after the last air display in September, it is often possible to accept outside work. Tasks to date are the refurbishment of Bristol Museum's Bristol Boxkite; the world's oldest DH60 Moth, owned by BAe (and now based here at Old Warden); all the fabric on the fuselage and flying surfaces on both our and the Battle of Britain Memorial Flight's Hurricane; the assembly of a privately-owned and rebuilt original Sopwith Camel to airworthy condition to be based at Old Warden; the rebuild of a set of Bristol Fighter wings and possibly the recover of a set of Puss Moth wings.

These, then, are the main areas of work. However, many other tasks are carried out. There is the consultant and parts procurement side for four aircraft being rebuilt for the Collection: the Shuttleworth Veteran Aeroplane Society is rebuilding Richard Shuttleworth's own Desoutter Monoplane and the original Blake Blue Tit at the Collection; the Northern Aeroplane Workshops are building a Bristol M1C monoplane to original drawings and specifications; and a joint venture between volunteers and the Imperial War Museum has almost completed the rebuild of the Collection's Hawker Sea Hurricane at Duxford.

Another area of winter work assuming greater importance is the job of drawing a basically complete engine out of store, and rebuilding it as a serviceable spare. This task obviously prevents the engine deteriorating further and holds a readily available engine spare, which can often be a display item. The Bristol Mercury 30 was such an engine, brought out of store and completely stripped, inspected and rebuilt, whilst the Mercury 8 plodded on in the Gladiator. A winter engine change-over reduced the number of flying days lost to a minimum. A similar idea was carried out on the Rolls-Royce Falcon III, brought in from display in hangar 4, completely stripped, inspected, crack checked, measured, re-assembled, painted and

Below and opposite: In the hangar the Hucks starter is used to test-turn the Hind's newly installed Kestrel engine before the aircraft is taken outside and fired up.

installed as a 'new' engine in our Bristol Fighter. The removed engine will undergo the same treatment but appears to require more rectification. Also rebuilt is a Gipsy Major, to be held either for the Magister or Tiger Moth, and the 80 and 110 hp le Rhône engine for the Sopwith Pup and Avro 504 respectively. A Genet engine is now almost complete and ready for the Southern Martlet, and there are still several applicable engines or parts of engines in store, waiting for treatment.

A question repeatedly asked, with no real answer, is: 'Where do the spares come from?' There is no one reply, because each shortage will lead an investigation up a totally different path and open up more unexplored possibilities. As a charity, the Collection is unable to meet the commercial cost of buying an available item, either new or second-hand, but over the years an excellent rapport has been established with many individuals, either in their private capacity or in industry. Investigations start in the stores at the Collection, where a number of assorted items have been amassed, all second-hand or scrap, and attempts will be made to salvage an item by carrying out whatever process or repair scheme is required to return it to an airworthy condition. In the past, items have been exchanged for those in private collections or museums, but these sources are dwindling, with widespread pillage by commercial projects. Several items are donated by friends of the Collection, and by advertising in the popular aviation press, often leading to energetic bartering. If all else fails, and it becomes necessary to have a part manufactured, often the sale of an unwanted item will raise funds that way. Many components, although no longer stock items, can still be made to pattern or drawing, as long as the correct material (or better) is available. Recent examples are valve springs, piston rings, brake cables, gaskets, wooden propellers, streamline and bracing wires, seals, fuel and oil tanks and cowlings.

As can be seen from all this, no two problems are similar as no two aircraft or engines are identical. Hopefully, each repair, rebuild, or refurbish, although carried out to standard aeronautical practice, will also have been carried out with such care, enthusiasm and sympathy for the task in hand, that it will last for a considerable length of time. Often this task cannot be carried out on a commercial basis — it just would not be cost effective. In this way, the Collection can add more airworthy aircraft to the fleet, hangar space permitting, without sacrificing the high standard of workmanship required.

7
What are they like to Fly —
and to Display?

There are several aircraft museums containing a host of very valuable machines that have numerous claims to historical fame, but by far the majority of these have been relegated to permanent roles as static exhibits. Clearly they play significant parts in aeronautical education, especially when easily accessible for viewing in city centres; there they are seen each year by thousands of schoolchildren, many of whom otherwise would know only the modern airliners in which they might be fortunate enough to fly on holiday.

The Shuttleworth Collection, however, is unique. The founder, Richard Shuttleworth, insisted that everything in his possession should be made to work as well as it had done when new. That policy has been continued throughout the Collection's existence and today the Old Warden hangars house the world's only range of airworthy historic aeroplanes dating from soon after the birth of manned flight to World War II.

Very few people are privileged to fly in any of these valuable aeroplanes, for the amount of flying must be kept to a practical minimum in order to reduce wear and tear on engines, airframes and associated components. With one or two exceptions, a Shuttleworth aeroplane takes to the air only when it needs a test flight or to give a public demonstration. A type such as the Sopwith Pup of 1916 with its short-life rotary engine flies about forty minutes in an average year; the earliest flying machines dating to before World War I do even less. But they are maintained in airworthy condition, to be on show each day as living examples of working machinery, with real oil falling onto real drip trays and a total absence of the dead atmosphere that surrounds an inert exhibit.

Clearly each type has its own characteristics and tends to display its own temperament. An early machine, with warping wings instead of ailerons to provide lateral control, may lack the positive response and 'feel' that we expect from the more conventionally-equipped types. The Bleriot, with its main wheels that castor in either direction, cannot be controlled on the ground without suitably knowledgeable help from people at the wingtips. The Boxkite must be flown within a very small limiting speed range and turns must be made without slip if height is not to be lost, therefore calling for careful planning when positioning for a display.

This is not the place to give detailed descriptions of the handling features of individual aircraft, as these appear in the companion volume *From Bleriot to Spitfire*, but a general explanation may interest. Few people can relate themselves in any way to one of the World's earliest flying machines, but many readers will be pilots and, even for those who have no practical flying experience, a description of a flight in a hypothetical light aeroplane of the late twenties or early thirties may stimulate the imagination.

Firstly, the weather must be right. The wind must be neither strong nor blustery, for the wing-loading of an early aeroplane will be low; this means that there is a fairly large area of lifting surface (wing) for a low total weight. Whilst this will affect its in-flight handling, it will be even more noticeable on the ground, when a gust of wind from one side will not only cause the machine to weathercock into the direction from which the air is blowing, but may lift the wing on that side and even cause the other wing to touch the ground — or worse. Next, the aerodrome must be suitable. Generally the length of available take-off or landing run is not a problem, but its direction is. Until the mid-thirties nearly all aeroplanes had relatively little directional control when on the ground, with fixed tailskids and no brakes, so a grass airfield that is as broad as it is long provides the ideal answer if operations are not to be stopped when the wind changes. If all take-offs and landings can be made precisely into wind, without the need to climb or approach over, or near to, gust-generating trees, then many of the problems disappear.

We are ready to fly. We have checked the documents and have accepted the aeroplane. Chocks are placed in front of the wheels, for while this is a wise precaution even on braked aeroplanes, on the brakeless veterans chocks are essential. Before climbing aboard, a pilot carries out an external pre-flight check, ensuring that there is no damage to the fabric, all cowlings are secure and their buttons properly closed, controls move freely, landing and flying wires are correctly tensioned, the propeller has no nicks and many other points of relevance to the safety of flight. This walk-round neither reduces the importance of the preparatory work carried out by the engineers, nor is it a reflection on their skills, but the pilot is wholly responsible for the aeroplane that he accepts to fly and minor damage could have occurred after the machine had been signed-out as technically serviceable and before the flight begins.

The pilot checks his equipment, such as ensuring that his goggles are clean and then mounts his machine, taking care where he treads. He satisfies himself that the cushions are correct for height and for his distance from the rudder pedals (although on some types these are adjustable) and he straps himself in tightly. This is very important, for after being aboard for a few minutes, when the cushions have settled, the straps always become looser than when first secured. Unlike those on modern machines, early harnesses cannot be adjusted without unfastening the entire package and starting again. This is a cumbersome procedure and is better completed while there are no other distractions, such as a running engine to handle.

Previous page: The Gladiator displays its upper surfaces turning around the unique and famous bend in the viewing enclosure at Old Warden.

Opposite: The Hawker Hind is one of the most popular performers at Old Warden displays.

The two most common starting procedures among aircraft of this era are the hand-swing and the use of a starter-magneto. Taking the first, which is more usual among the lighter types, we have relatively few checks to complete, for cockpits of the time have remarkably few moving controls. Petrol on, ignition switches off and throttle closed are the pilot's actions before the engineer floods the carburettor and turns the engine through about four compressions to suck the fuel into the system. Then, with the stick hard back to prevent the tail from lifting off the ground, the pilot responds to the words 'throttle set — contact' by inching the lever slightly forwards, turning on the switch(es) and repeating the same words. When the propeller is swung by hand, he makes every endeavour to 'catch' the engine as it fires and he gently manipulates the throttle to establish a smooth warm-up setting in the region of 800-1000 rpm. Immediately he checks that the oil pressure is rising. This is perhaps the most important cockpit information available to a pilot and if the pressure fails to increase quickly, he switches off the engine to avoid possible damage through lack of lubrication. Here a pilot requires specialist knowledge of the type, for required oil pressure figures vary from as little as 5-8 lb for a splash-fed system to more than 80 lb for the average radial.

The alternative starting method, commonly found on Armstrong-Siddeley radials such as the Mongoose in the Hawker Tomtit and the Lynx in the Avro Tutor, but also on the V-8 Airdisco on the DH 51, is by use of a starter-magneto. As a part of airworthiness approval all aero engines are required to have fully duplicated ignition, with two magnetos and with two sparking plugs in each cylinder, but in effect this method includes a third ignition switch connected to a hand-cranked (third) magneto, operated by the pilot, while an engineer winds on the outside to rotate the engine. To ensure that both parties wind at the same time, the order is 'one, two, three — go', leading to quite energetic exercise for both. The third switch is turned off as soon as everything is running smoothly.

An aero-engine requires a gentle warming-up period, the length depending on the temperature of the day and whether it was a start from cold. If so, even in warm weather, almost five minutes should be allowed to ensure that the oil is not too viscous to be circulating fully before the power is increased for magneto checks. Some engines have oil temperature gauges and on a really cold day twelve minutes can elapse before the minimum operating figure shows on the dial. The warm-up and subsequent running on the ground should not be performed with the engine idling, for this tends to cause plug-fouling, so a compromise setting in the region of 1000 rpm is about right for most machines. This time is not wasted, however, for the pilot carries out checks on instruments, flying controls, trimmer and other essentials for safe flight.

After the engine checks, the chocks can be waved away and taxying begins. This is where we find one of the first main differences in required technique between the ancient and the modern. The older 'tail-dragger' has its nose well above the horizon and therefore offers no view directly forward, so the pilot must weave from side-to-side throughout the ground manoeuvring stage, swinging the nose to the left and looking to the right to check the ground ahead and then vice-versa; but an aeroplane with a tailskid fixed to the sternpost and with no brakes may not always move readily in the required direction. It has a strong desire always to head into wind, so to oppose that natural inclination it may be necessary to use a careful burst of throttle to move some air past the rudder in order to achieve any directional response. However, this calls for caution in two other ways; rapid throttle opening may make the tail lift (possibly causing the propeller to nick the ground, with expensive consequences) and any increase in power will cause the speed to rise, with no brakes available to prevent the machine running away. A part of the vintage art that has died with modernity is the use of ailerons to help to activate a turn; for example, when travelling downwind, an up-going aileron will catch the wind from behind and will help to move that side forward or vice-versa when taxying into wind. In confined spaces or when the wind is energetic, wingtip men are essential; they are not just there for the walk (or trot) but must pull back when on the inside of a turn and must remember to release the pressure before the aircraft reaches the desired new heading, or it will continue well past the pilot's intended direction. Without brakes, taxying downwind or downhill calls for a completely closed throttle, which in turn can lead to plug problems!

We have reached the downwind end of the aerodrome and we carry out some straightforward but very important pre-take-off checks, amounting mainly to the trim setting, fuel (on and sufficient), oil pressure, hatches, harness and goggles. Here a final dead-cut ignition check is wise, followed by a thorough search all round (especially in the direction of the landing approach) to see that all is clear, but this is a fundamental decision time, especially with a valuable historic aeroplane. If the oil pressure is in doubt, or the engine is not as smooth as it was last time, or the wind is freshening beyond expectations, or for any reason there is not total cockpit contentment, that essential sense of responsibility must always dictate the next move. It is far better to abandon the flight before it begins, to ensure another chance, rather than to regret an unwise decision a little later, even if this entails disappointing a crowd at a flying display. To turn round and taxy back in such a circumstance may be difficult, but probably the aeroplane is the world's last airworthy specimen of its type. The pilot is captain of his own ship; he has been entrusted with a very special piece of machinery and he must act accordingly.

We will assume, though, that all is well and we are ready to go. After a final look round inside the cockpit and another check outside in all directions, we move forwards gently to align the aeroplane into wind; then we run ahead slowly for a few yards before opening the throttle, smoothly but fully, easing the stick carefully forwards to raise the tail to improve the directional control by putting the rudder more fully into the airflow. During this stage, and especially due to the gyroscopic effect as the tail rises, energetic footwork may be needed in order to keep straight against the torque and propeller slipstream effects, but as the forward speed increases all the controls become more effective and the movements must be reduced progressively. Some machines fly themselves off when ready and few need more than a gentle back pressure to take to the air.

There are various techniques for the climb. Some pilots raise the nose fairly soon after lift-off to establish a steepish climb angle, but this means that the airspeed will be relatively low, with ineffective flying controls, the chance of inadequate engine cooling and the worst possible forward view; also if the engine should fail at an early stage in the climb, the chances of recovery are slim. A more shallow angle and higher airspeed, though, will reduce the rate of climb, so clearly a compromise is wise, but in the case of an historic aeroplane safety and sense must take precedence over performance.

Rudder plays a very significant part in handling a biplane. During the climb, considerable pressure on one pedal must be maintained in order to achieve and sustain balanced flight, the amount depending on the speed and power used and the appropriate side depending on the direction of rotation of the engine and propeller. Even in level flight, rudder must be used throughout if the needles of the turn and slip indicator are to show balanced flight.

Below: Times change: nowadays it is not legal to carry passengers during displays, and for many years the Shuttleworth Collection has been a leader in setting this example.

On many modern aeroplanes, a tolerable (if not very accurate) turn can be achieved by aileron alone, but in our earlier machine sideways stick movement may introduce the required bank but no rate of turn, or even possibly a change of heading in the wrong direction! This is because a downgoing aileron generates more drag than its opposite number. The problem is most marked with the very early designs, on which the downgoing control moves as far as the other moves up, thus creating excessive aileron drag. Later types have differential ailerons, with the upward movement more pronounced than the downward travel, but even with these aids a turn without the use of adequate rudder can be a most ineffective and uncomfortable activity. The best way for a pilot to acquire the art and feel of balanced flight is to practise turns from one direction to the other without pausing in between, but checking the position of the top needle throughout the exercise.

With appropriate respect for their ages, many Shuttleworth aeroplanes are not cleared to perform aerobatic manoeuvres. However some may be looped and one or two are rolled, so long as a positive loading is retained throughout. In the main, a biplane flies round a loop fairly readily, with a need for varying rudder pressures throughout to compensate for changes in the combination of power in relation to airspeed. Some biplanes, though, are reluctant to roll, with the added problem of aileron drag to make the manoeuvre a critical performance. Aerobatics, however, are not essential for the enjoyment of pure flying. An open cockpit, the splendid isolation of being alone in the sky with no radio to disturb one's peace of mind and a newly-mown all grass aerodrome are some of the ingredients in the best of the freedom of flight.

One aspect that is of considerable concern to a pilot and of interest to a spectator is the landing. Again, many a modern nosewheel machine can be set-up on a steady, powered approach and it is possible (though not correct) to continue this state until the mainwheels touch, then to close the throttle and later apply the brakes. This may be a slight over-simplification, but such machines have been landed quite safely in that manner! Not so, though, with the classic tail-dragging brakeless biplane; here a well-organized approach is essential, a landing path into wind should be selected and the final stages should be made at a predetermined airspeed with stick loads trimmed out. If the approach is too high, there are no flaps to act as drag-producing barn doors, so sideslipping is the only way in which the surplus height can be shed. This is an art that few pilots practise — and no one learns — today, but on the glide one wing is lowered and opposite rudder is applied to prevent the nose from falling, therefore presenting much more aeroplane into the oncoming airflow and causing a steeper descent without an embarrassing increase in airspeed. When the desired glide path is reached again, the wings are levelled and the rudder centralized to resume a normal glide, but the change of flight condition must be completed at a safe height; this is to avoid either sideslipping into the ground or causing too many tasks to be carried out at the same time, for the airspeed, height and angle of hold-off are critical if a tidy and safe landing is to be achieved on all three points.

A pilot should look well ahead when landing any type of aircraft, but his point of vision is more critical with a tail-dragger, as he must assess the correct angle at which to touch down by relation to the amount of nose that appears above the horizon. This varies vastly from one type to another, so it is wise to have a mental picture of the amount of aeroplane that you require to see ahead. The airspeed at the start of the hold-off and the rate at which this is performed are equally critical, for either too high a figure or too rapid a round-out (or, worse still, both!) will cause the aircraft to gain height and then 'sit up and beg' with a rapid loss of both airspeed and control. Too late or too gentle a hold-off, though, is less punitive, for this can be converted into a safe if possibly untidy landing on the mainwheels only, provided that the tail has been lowered sufficiently to ensure adequate ground clearance for the propeller. On some types, though, this clearance is small and a virtual three-pointer is almost essential.

Once an aeroplane is on the ground on all three points, the only causes for it to become airborne again are a patch of rough ground or a severe gust. Such an unexpected excursion into the air is not a handling fault by the pilot. With a wheel landing, though, the pilot must take care not to ease the stick back until the tail is ready to go down of its own accord, for in this case the machine has been placed on the ground at something more than the minimum flying speed, so it is ready to take to the air again briefly at the slightest touch of pilot provocation. Obviously some aircraft are easier than others to place neatly onto three points, while all are susceptible to the effects of the conditions of the moment. In a calm, most machines can be positioned accurately onto the ground with a gentle but satisfying 'clunk', but strong and especially gusty winds can play havoc with any pilot's best-laid plans. In such circumstances, or if it is necessary to land out of wind, an intentional wheeler is a cautious move.

Another significant difference between a tail-down and a nosewheel type concerns the nature of the landing run. Apart from a need to prevent over-running the end of the airfield (for, with less aerodynamic drag in its level ground attitude a 'trike' tends to roll further) the more modern machine calls for relatively little pilot attention. On a three point landing, though, smart reactions may be necessary, especially as the speed decreases and the lowered rudder has very little passing airflow to make it effective. Here, a complete calm can be more embarrassing than a gentle steady wind, for just prior to stopping, with no brakes and virtually no moving air, even rapid and maximum rudder deflection may have little effect. This is the time at which a swing is most likely to start, with the pilot having the minimum chance of being able to prevent it from developing into a ground loop. The problem is accentuated on a tail-down type because, to make the tail of the aircraft sit on the ground, the centre of gravity must be behind the main wheels, so when a swing starts, the momentum is such that the bulk of the aircraft's weight tends to push ahead and aggravate the swing. By this stage the pilot may be wise to admit temporary defeat, for he will have little control over whether the aeroplane comes gradually to a gentle halt or whether the turn tightens sufficiently severely to cause a side-strain on the undercarriage or even cause the outside wing to dip into the ground. While most flight phases should be in the control of the pilot, this situation must be accepted as one of the less happy moments in the life of anyone who flies tail-dragging (and especially brakeless) historic aeroplanes. Fortunately serious groundloops are rare, but they do and will happen — even to the best!

We will assume that the landing, if not perfect, has ended normally. The flight as such may be over, but the sortie is not. The aircraft must be returned safely to dispersal, using wingtip handlers if the type and/or conditions make it wise to do so. It must be parked correctly and sensibly, remembering that unaided turns cannot be made in confined spaces and that there are no brakes with which to stop. Finally, although most people remember to warm and run-up engines before flying, many tend to overlook the need for careful handling at the end. Types vary, but to ensure even cooling and to clear the plugs after taxying, most power units should be given a steady run-down for two or three minutes before switching off.

After turning off the fuel, ensuring that **all** switches are off and completing any other post-flight checks, a pilot should have a few words with an engineer to discuss any points that may be relevant. Was the oil pressure steady throughout the flight? Were there any rough spots on the engine at any power setting? Was the rigging right with the wings level in stick central/hands off cruising flight? A previous pilot had reported a sticking gauge; had the action taken cured this? If anything of special significance was noticed this should be recorded in writing, for tendencies over several flights, probably by different pilots, could tell a tale that might prevent trouble developing in the future.

Apart from entering the flight details in the authorization book, the pilot has completed the exercise. He can relax and think back. Perhaps he has just flown the world's sole surviving specimen of a famous historic type; both before and during the trip he was aware of the responsibility that

goes with this. It should not have prevented him from deriving his ration of pleasure, but only now can he savour the full effects of vintage-style aviation. One experienced pilot stated that flying was really enjoyable only in retrospect, but that the pleasures of taking the thoughts of the day's flight to the evening armchair, or to the bath, far outweighed any of the worries that may have arisen during the trip itself; but this is another story. The problems and pleasures associated with aeroplanes and flying warrant a special book and this is not the place to reminisce.

* * *

This brief description of a local sortie in an historic aeroplane may come to life more fully if we consider now a typical demonstration flight, for this is what many thousands of visitors come to Old Warden to see. Some people travel for literally hundreds of miles to watch their chosen aeroplanes in the air and the organizers and pilots are aware of the various wishes of different groups of spectators. Some come to take still photographs, others concentrate on video recording, while another group concentrates on making sound recordings of engine starting, or of various power settings in flight, or the crackle that some exhausts emit when the throttle is fully closed. These and the wishes of the majority, who wish just to see the machines in the air at close quarters and others who are anxious to hear historical detail over the public address system, are fed into a display pattern that must be dictated primarily by the needs of flight safety.

Preliminary planning for any but the smallest flying display must begin many months before the day of the event, but from a flying angle a pilot is concerned only from the morning of the show. He will have his aircraft allocated to him and he will begin to consider whether the conditions are likely to affect the nature of his demonstration. If the wind is light and conditions are smooth, he knows that he will have scope to present the machine accurately and manoeuvres will be possible within easy view of the crowd. If there are gusts, he will need added height and may need to make only gently-banked turns avoiding known areas of turbulence. The decision is based not solely on wind strength, for rough-riding thermal activity can occur when the windsock is well below the horizontal.

Before the show starts, all pilots attend a detailed briefing on the afternoon's plan. The weather, any local restrictions or unusual activities are discussed, timings agreed and questions answered. There may be doubts about which grass runway to use, for one heading may suit one type that needs to operate into wind and another may be more suitable for a second machine that requires a longer run. However, these and other matters are resolved, with the proviso that if weather conditions should change just before or during the display, final discussions will take place on the flight line.

The show has begun. We are the third item on the programme and we have an allocation of seven minutes in the air. This could be critical, for the next performer is a visiting aircraft that is operating on an overhead time slot, so if for any reason we should be a minute late in beginning the demonstration, we must reduce our time by this amount unless there has been a mutual pre-flight agreement with all other parties concerned.

The second aircraft in the display is on the far side of the airfield, at the take-off holding point, with two minutes to go, so with ten minutes before our public performance begins it is time for us to be aboard our machine. We must allow for the possibility of a hesitant starter, with adequate time for an unhurried warm-up and run-up and for taxying out while the previous machine is before the crowd. Just as we are about to wave away the chocks, we receive a message that item number four will be two minutes late on the overhead slot; we should absorb this by delaying our take-off until the previous machine has landed and cleared the runway and then extend our airborne performance by one minute. We plan how to use this extra time effectively and safely whilst we are taxying to the take-off point.

We are there. The wind is blowing steadily at about ten knots almost straight down the runway. Good. The previous aircraft is positioning on final approach, lands very tidily, runs straight without undue effort by the pilot because of the convenient wind direction and clears to the right to avoid the need to cross the duty runway whilst taxying back. A glance round the circuit to ensure that there are no intruders, an especial check that the approach is clear, a glance at air traffic control from which a steady green light is trained on us and away we go. Safety before spectacle is the order, so we climb gently ahead over the college sports field to gain airspeed before beginning a turn round the clump of trees, taking care to keep the Home Farm well clear on the outside, leading to a straight run-in, almost downwind along the front but well clear of the public enclosure fence. Not too low, for then only the people in the front would see; but too high and the effect is lost. Just under half throttle, a quick glance at the oil pressure and a gentle power increase before completing a moderately banked right-hand turn inside the north end of the airfield, through 360°, then continuing ahead over an empty stretch of the overflow car park on the north side of the Biggleswade road. A slight gain in height is advisable here before a carefully positioned left-hand turn round the trees of the coach park, to begin another flypast from beside the blister hangar, along the first part of the NW-SE grass runway; then, with ample airspeed in hand after descending again from the turn round the trees, a steepish right-hand level

turn round the outside of the display flight line, well outboard of the air traffic control building to conform to separation minima laid down by the Civil Aviation Authority, but close enough for the cameras to click successfully. The view of the upper surface of the aircraft that this manoeuvre provides seems to be the most popular for spectators and photographers alike.

Still we have some airspeed in hand and we are facing into wind, so we increase power again, raise the nose, and with a quick oil pressure and time check (three and a half minutes to go) carry out a gentle wing-over to the left. This places us near the upwind end of the field, from which we descend downwind along the front of the enclosure again to carry out a steepish climbing turn to the right over the Biggleswade road hedge towards the bridge; but instead of repeating a full wing-over, we level our nose at the highest point heading up the NE-SW runway, which gives us an ideal position and a low airspeed from which to make a well-throttled-back minimum-speed flypast. We have left this until a late stage in the demonstration, for by now we are satisfied that there is virtually no turbulence, no windshear nor any other meteorological trap for the pilot who flies both low and slow.

We are at the upwind end and have remained at a constant 200 feet in our slow run. More power, another tightish turn round the tree clump and a final fastish run downwind leading into a sustained level steep turn to the right, inside the manoeuvring area of the airfield, finishing after 450°, heading over the windsock to the east (checking: one minute left) for a run straight into a shortened, close-in downwind leg, short base and then a landing approach from a short final position. But alas, we have slightly overestimated the wind strength and we need to slip-off some height, but this is no worry for it is an impressive vintage-style manoeuvre and could well have been an intentional part of the display. No one will know otherwise, although a few pilots might guess and one or two will probably say so. Apart from this minor misjudgement, with calm conditions and a well-mannered aeroplane, the sequence has worked well. Now there is just the landing left to do. Just? This is the one time at which eyes and voices (qualified and otherwise) are at their most critical. Every pilot knows it. With thousands of people in the viewing enclosure we are aware that a hash-up here will be seen, noted and remembered to the extent that any reasonable demonstration flying that may have gone before it will be forgotten immediately. We try hard, but not too hard, for only a relaxed pilot lands well. We touch quite smoothly, but with the tailskid slightly off the ground in what is called a tail-down wheeler.

Opposite: Long shadows show that work continues long past the end of a display.

Acceptable, perhaps, but really a sideslipping approach should be followed by a three-pointer. Although other pilots might notice, fortunately the non-flying members of the audience react only to bounces or ballooning, so we are safe from scorn.

The landing run is dead straight, the credit for which must go to the wind blowing down the runway, but we are slightly self-critical at failing to land precisely as we intended and this could spoil any post-flight feeling of contentment. However, just as we have turned off the strip at the end of our landing run, item four in the programme flies steadily overhead, leaving no gap between the display acts. Was our precise timing through luck, or careful judgement? To compensate for the wheely landing we credit ourself with the latter; and we are happy again.

Although the description of a typical demonstration flight refers to the need for precise timing throughout an event, some of the shows at Old Warden are on a more unhurried basis, to bring back the atmosphere of the informal 'open days' held in the sixties. On these occasions each historic aeroplane starts, taxies, flies and returns to the flight line without any other machine moving. These smaller events are interspersed with a number of large full-scale displays or pageants, therefore providing facilities for visitors of all tastes.

Since 1 April 1989 it has become necessary for a display organizer to seek and obtain permission from the Civil Aviation Authority to run a show; also, every pilot flying a civil aeroplane in such an event is required to hold a CAA display authorization, valid both for the category of aircraft that he flies and for the nature of the proposed demon-stration, i.e. flypasts, formation or aerobatics. A show organizer is required to pay a substantial fee for the privilege of being monitored and only a very small event, at which fewer than 500 people are expected to attend, is exempt from these requirements. This change was introduced on the instructions of the Department of Transport — the CAA's 'owners' — because of a perceived need for the Authority to exercise tighter control over the display movement.

* * *

Before moving away from the art of vintage flight, perhaps we should explain that the pilot of an historic aeroplane is not necessarily better or more qualified than one who flies the modern 'tin trike'. The requirements are different. An early aeroplane calls for more in the way of handling and airmanship skills, but there are no avionics or other electronic devices to master; the later machine is much less tricky to fly, but may have radio navigation equipment that permits operation in controlled airspace, with aids for letting-down to a major airport in bad weather and other items from modern technology that call for special training and skills. In short, the older aeroplane is essentially something that provides satisfaction to the pilot for the pleasure of pure flying, while the product of recent years is a very practical travel tool for anyone who is qualified to use the resources that it is able to offer. The difference is as interesting as it is marked; but this writer knows which of the two switches him on!

8
A Display Day

It is a summer Sunday; the clock on the tower of the Shuttleworth Agricultural College has just struck eight. Already the doors of several hangars are open, for this is the start of a day to be devoted to Service aeroplanes from 1910 onwards. A handful of engineers and a pair of volunteer helpers are on the move with the Gladiator and the Tutor, whilst a couple of others are clearing the way to extract the LVG CV1 and Pup of World War I from their hangar spaces. The aerodrome is reasonably dry and the windsock is moving only gently, so conditions at this early hour seem well suited to a successful day's flying. Soon the home-based aeroplanes will be parked along the viewing enclosure fence to form the nucleus of the display flight line.

The first visitors are waiting patiently outside the aerodrome gates, each hoping to benefit from a crack-of-dawn start by obtaining a front row in the main viewing enclosure. One puts forward an excuse to be allowed in, showing a rather suspect press identity, but without a Shuttleworth press ticket or early pass he is asked to go back into the queue with the others. He feels that it was worth a try. Along the line of early stalwarts, the variety of brogues tells the true tale of enthusiasm for the happenings at Old Warden; a car load has driven overnight from Perth and another has just arrived from North Wales. Even more clearly apparent are the tongues from the far side of the Atlantic, for American aviation buffs (as they call themselves) just must come to see little old Shuttleworth. Before

Below: A unique line-up of historic aeroplanes awaiting the start of a Display Day.

long, the first coach has joined the queue, for this is a fast-growing mode of travel to displays, with associations, societies and firms' social clubs coming *en masse* from all over Britain. Two binocular-laden cyclists have placed themselves in readiness to jump the car queue and to take full advantage of their space-saving manoeuvrability when the gates are opened.

Whilst this growing and welcome mass of expectant enthusiasm may be mentally singing 'Why are we waiting?', the activity on the inside is growing in intensity. Car parkers are being briefed on the special requirements of the day; tickets and petty cash are being issued to the gate party; visiting stall-holders are preparing their wares for presentation to the public; Shuttleworth sales staff and programme sellers are making final arrangements to face the onslaught; a suspect drain is being checked and cleared to minimize the risk of trouble later in the day; and security arrangements are being finalized, with especial attention to the points of access to the airfield manoeuvring area. In an upstairs office the telephones ring incessantly.

Most of the essential participants in the overall scheme have started their duties that morning, for many are part-timers with other occupations, who devote these Sundays to the cause; the earlier preparatory arrangements have been carried out in the preceding days by members of the Collection's staff. But on the operational side, preliminary plans for the day may have been laid nearly a year previously; specific requests for demonstrations by Service aircraft must have been lodged with the Ministry of Defence by the first week in September of the previous year; permission must be obtained from the Civil Aviation Authority; the Airspace Utilisation Section of the National Air Traffic Service must have provided the required flight clearances; insurance, budgeting, publicity and other administrative angles must have been finalized long beforehand; and the detailed flying programme must have been prepared and circulated to all concerned in time for any problems to be raised, sorted and cleared well before the event. Today the displays consultant prepares the programme and hands over the running of the event to the duty pilot, who is one of the Shuttleworth pilots; this is arranged on a roster basis agreed in advance with the CAA.

The day itself shows little more than the tip of the organizational iceberg, but still many tasks remain, for some cannot be completed in advance. Perhaps the most significant of these is the effect of the weather on the programme, so fairly early in the morning the meteorological forecast is obtained via the Airmet Service; this provides the relevant information such as wind strengths and directions, cloud types, heights and amounts, whether icing is likely (it does not disappear in the summer), visibility (which, surprisingly, often does), whether rain is likely and details of the general situation; the concern extends not just around the Old Warden circuit, for aircraft are scheduled to appear on overhead slot times from as far apart as Royal Air Force Lossiemouth in Morayshire and the Royal Naval Air Station at Culdrose in Cornwall. Unexpected winds or bad weather en route, even with perfect conditions at each end, can play tricks with the timings of overhead appearances.

On this occasion the forecast seems generally reasonable, with acceptable levels of cloud and visibility, but with one headache; the wind might increase in strength to eighteen knots with gusts to twenty-five. Forecast winds cannot always be precise and the overall trend can be affected by local variations, so this presents a planning problem that cannot be resolved until the allotted times at which the more wind-critical aircraft are due to perform. Almost certainly the Bristol Boxkite, scheduled in the show to represent the very beginning of military aviation, will be unable to fly; for safety, it will stay in its hangar. The marginal cases, though, are outside already and the engineers are warned of the threatened wind so that they can prepare to tie them down; these include both the 1916 Sopwith Pup and the 1918 LVG CV1, each of which becomes difficult to manage in rough conditions. The decision to fly or not to fly is based not only on the strength of the wind, but also on its stability; a **steady** wind of fifteen knots or so may be perfectly manageable, whereas a strength in single figures can produce blustery conditions and unacceptable vertical air movement. One of the display pilots has just air-tested the 1929 Hawker Tomtit

Energetic action is required to start the engines of the Bristol Fighter (left) and the DH 51 (right).

and he reports that so far the wind is no problem; but it is too early to assess the likely state of play for the afternoon.

The gates are open and the early-morning enthusiasts have found their chosen parking and viewing spots. The initial queue has been cleared and only a few isolated visitors are coming in, for there is a noticeable gap between the 'dawn patrol' and the general run of spectators, many of whom endeavour to enter the aerodrome at the same time and then wonder why there are delays. Despite words of advice put over on press releases and in advertisements, advising people to come early, relatively few heed this and a fresh queue develops. The gate crews and car parkers work as hard as possible to keep everything and everyone moving, but only one or two individuals raising queries, or not having their money ready on arrival at the entrance, can generate lengthy tailbacks that become very difficult to clear. The senior car parker calls on the walkie-talkie system to say that the main enclosures are nearly full and the overflow park on the opposite side of the Biggleswade road must be brought into use when a further 100 cars have been admitted. This changeover creates temporary difficulties as people are needed to handle traffic and occupants at both entry points at the same time; the switch from one park to the other calls for a form of military precision.

Throughout this time visiting aircraft have been arriving from all over Britain and the continent. Prior permission is required, as on an occasion such as this the demand may exceed the supply; the available parking area is limited, and to conform to both Ministry of Defence and Civil Aviation Authority requirements, adequate clearances must be maintained between the display line (used by pilots as a positioning guide for their demonstrations) and all obstructions. In this context a parked aeroplane or the edge of the public viewing enclosure constitutes just such an obstruction, so careful advanced planning includes a severe restriction on the number of non-participating visiting aircraft that can be allowed to land.

In addition to the spectators who come by air, several visiting display aircraft are arriving. One of the Royal Navy's two surviving Fairey Swordfish has plodded slowly from Yeovilton in Somerset; the Beaver preserved by the Army Air Corps arrived early, but has just landed back from a local reconnoitre of the display area; a private Harvard, flying in military markings by permission of the authorities, is marshalled into place. Authenticity is a keyword among those who take a serious view of aircraft preservation and the markings, lettering and colour schemes are very important.

Midday strikes. The commentator makes a few introductory announcements and reminds all display participants that they must attend the flying briefing at 12.30. This is a firm requirement and only in very rare circumstances can absence be accepted; in that case written and telephone instructions must have been given beforehand and agreed.

Briefing begins. The weather forecast is read and discussed. Clearly it is not possible yet to make firm decisions regarding some of the aircraft, so the final yes/no verdict will be agreed on the flight line; but with several participants due to appear on fixed overhead slot times, flexibility will be difficult to accommodate. As a result, several of the sequences are reshuffled to minimize the effect of last-minute flight cancellations and a revised version of the operational programme is issued. At this late stage any changes must be worked round the pre-agreed timings of visiting participants so that their slots remain unaffected.

Below: Refuelling also is hard work.

Although most of the pilots present have performed at Old Warden on many occasions and all are experienced display performers, the basic rules must be explained at every event. The Old Warden regulations are kept to a realistic minimum, based on many years of experience of the particular display site, but these have been modified slightly to include the Civil Aviation Authority's laid-down minimum distances from crowds, buildings and parked aircraft. There are many positive guidelines regarding taxying paths, holding points whilst awaiting clearance to take-off, headings and positions of flypasts, the importance of keeping the operational area clear in case the pilot of a performing machine needs to land prematurely, sensitive areas that should not be overflown, action to take in the event of an engine being reluctant to start at the allotted minute and many others. Watches are checked and all are reminded of the need to keep to time. An early slippage of a minute can have repercussive effects throughout the display and could create an unacceptable hazard if a pilot on an overhead slot is unable to make radio contact before his initial run-in. All-round discipline plays a key role in the safety of any show and a participant who may wish to do anything unusual must ask and obtain permission during (not after!) the briefing, so that everyone likely to be affected (the controller, the marshallers, the next performer, the commentator *et al*) knows what to expect. Imagine the irretrievable delay if a pilot of a non-radio aircraft completes his act and, instead of landing back at the allotted minute, flies straight on to return to his home base. No one is sure if he is flying away to build-up speed or height for a final fast run-past and by the time that his intentions become self-explanatory, a minute or more has been lost. Hence the importance of briefing as the hard core of the day's programme. It is one of the numerous background activities that take place before, during and after the event to help to ensure that the display is smooth and enjoyable for those who have to come to see it — and, above all, that it is safe in all possible respects. A well-worn expression at Shuttleworth briefings is that whenever in doubt, safety must take precedence over spectacle.

Because of this need for safety and to ensure the minimum practical wear and tear on the historic aeroplanes, the pilots chosen to fly Shuttleworth aircraft in displays are vetted very carefully — and their subsequent performance is monitored throughout. Bad engine handling, undue stress on an airframe, opting to fly in conditions that should have dictated cancellation, or failure to require a wingtip handler when taxying in windy conditions or in a confined space are among the signs that a person may not be quite to the standard expected. So pilots are selected not only for their abilities to fly accurately (important though this is) but because of their attitudes towards the responsibilities involved in being entrusted with some of the world's most valuable and irreplaceable historic aircraft. In short, airmanship in its broadest sense.

No rigid qualifications are laid down for admission to the small band of selected Shuttleworth pilots. In addition to the importance of attitude and outlook, a varied flying background is essential. All have been trained in the Services and most are either current or former test pilots or flying instructors — or both. The numbers are kept to a practical minimum to ensure that each obtains some level of continuity. If an aeroplane flies only six times in a year, clearly it should be flown three times each by two pilots and not by six different people each having to undergo refamiliarization for one annual sortie on the type. Training time is expensive in wear on engine and airframe components and must be restricted to flights that are unavoidable.

The show is scheduled to begin at 1400. A few minutes before this the controller is in radio contact with the RAF pilot of the Tornado, who confirms that he is on target time and will come in low and fast at the allotted moment. He does. Some say that a new, noisy aircraft such as this is out of place among the rural scenery of Old Warden, but others like to see a comprehensive display covering both the ancient and the modern. In an attempt to satisfy both viewpoints, two clearly defined patterns of display have been introduced: all-embracing functions such as the one forming the basis of this chapter and old-style informal and unhurried 'flying occasions' devoted exclusively to the earlier eras of aviation.

Below: One of two Fairey Swordfish operated by the Royal Navy Historic Flight leads the Collection's Hind and Gladiator prior to a unique formation flypast.

On this occasion the programme is not geared to any particular historical order, but rather in terms of performance contrasts. Although the forecast wind caused several possible alterations to be planned, fortunately the local conditions stabilised nearly an hour before the show started and, on a fingers-crossed basis, the original and more purposeful sequence was reinstated. So as the Tornado crosses the upwind boundary of the airfield on its final run, the LVG CV1, that slow but steady observation aircraft used by the Imperial German Air Force in 1918, receives a steady green light and lumbers slowly into the air. This gives viewers an instant reminder of the progress made in seventy years of aircraft development.

Many others follow. Each type has its band of supporters; some visitors may have flown or worked on machines that later became their favourites; later, because time makes memory into a very selective process. One may have been compelled to sweat for hours in very hot (or suffer in cold and wet) conditions trying to cure an ever-elusive snag when wanting to get away for a date, but these times of distress tend to fade compared with those magic moments when an aeroplane is all that it should be — and more. This, surely, must be part of the basis on which the growing interest in historic aeroplanes is built? Yet many of the keenest supporters have had no experience in flying, building or maintaining any machine. So what is the root of the attraction?

Below: Engineers preparing to hold down the tail for an engine run-up on the DH 51.

Whatever the cause, the next aeroplane in the programme can claim one of the biggest bands of followers: the Gloster Gladiator. Entering service in 1937 to become the RAF's last-ever biplane fighter, the Gladiator appeals to almost everyone. Certainly it is an impressive performer and one that is in demand at displays away from Old Warden as well as at home; but as with all Shuttleworth aeroplanes, its flying must be severely rationed and normally it departs to distant places only four or five times in a year. This restriction accentuates the difference between 'home' and 'away' events, for only at Old Warden can visitors see a whole package of historic aircraft in one event in one afternoon.

The aim throughout is to present to visitors a show that flows smoothly from one item to the next. Sometimes an event runs as though on rails and little energetic conducting is required; yet, on another occasion, setbacks build-up from the beginning and every ounce of available energy and a clear head are needed to produce any form of worthwhile sequence. Obviously, known weather problems can be predictable hazards to success, but often there is no easily definable reason for an event running well or badly. It cannot be forecast; more surprisingly, the cause may not be clear even in a calm analytical rundown afterwards.

The show is running more successfully than was anticipated — so far; in this case, one leading reason is clear, for the threatened wind has not developed and there are no weather-related causes for cancellations or delays. The Magister, though, refused to start as promptly as it should, but the pilot began his preparations in good time and the decision about the sortie is taken sufficiently early to signal to the pilot of the Harvard to perform one act ahead of schedule. Even allowing for the essential engine-warming period, everything happens slickly and, at take-off, he is only thirty seconds behind the Magister's allotted time. The Harvard loses this amount from his performing slot and the show is back on schedule.

While this change was being conducted on the flight line, the controller had received a telephone call to warn him that the Spitfire Vb from the Battle of Britain Memorial Flight had developed a slight coolant leak and would not be appearing. The Lancaster and Hurricane, however, were en route and a reorganized performance duration (fifteen minutes had been allotted for all three) could be agreed over the VHF radio with the formation leader in the Lancaster. A few words each way and agreement is reached for twelve minutes. Whilst nostalgia (and whatever the equivalent may be for the younger generations) worked overtime among the spectators, with the four synchronized Rolls-Royce Merlins of the Lancaster draining a little damp from the eyes of some of the hardiest on the field, a little more planning was underway with the home-based pilots. There were three extra minutes to be used, but only three, as after the next two aircraft an RAF Hawk would be on a fixed overhead slot and for fuel reserve reasons this could not be delayed. So it would not be practicable to add another aircraft into the available time and a compromise solution was agreed with the pilots concerned; each would add one minute to his sequence and, instead of starting to roll forwards when the first machine was on the base leg of the circuit, the second would delay his take-off until the first had landed and cleared the runway. It worked well and there was no recognizable gap in the programme.

So the show proceeded. Although conditions were better than anticipated, local low-level turbulence was enough to keep the Boxkite indoors. However, visitors were not to be disappointed, for the programme closed with a performance by the Collection's 1937 Hawker Hind light bomber that was restored over several years following a journey of 6,000 miles from Afghanistan. This large and powerful biplane and the crackle of its Rolls-Royce Kestrel engine combine to provide a very strong appeal to visitors. Not only is it the only Hind flying anywhere in the world, but it is the only airworthy example of the entire range of famous Hawker biplanes that formed the front-line mainstays of the Royal Air Force in the thirties.

Below: The Lynx engine on the Avro Tutor is fired into life by the Hucks starter.

The display is over, but activities are not. More than fifty visiting aircraft are preparing to depart and for half-an-hour or so the usually quiet rural aerodrome becomes one of the busiest airfields in Britain. At one time twenty-three aircraft are counted in the take-off queue, but all get away smartly with guidance from the marshallers' bats and under the careful eye of the duty controller, who releases them at the shortest safe interval between machines. To ensure this smooth and rapid departure flow, regulations forbid any pilot to land back (except in emergency) for one hour after the end of the show.

Not only are aeroplanes leaving, but the road-borne crowds are winding their ways home. Many cannot resist the bumper-to-bumper conditions that must prevail immediately the flying demonstrations have finished, but some stay back for a while; for a picnic, a final walk round the exhibition hangars, a meal in the aerodrome restaurant, or just a final stare at the unique line-up of living examples of aviation's past. At the same time, though, those who made the afternoon possible are still busy closing down the day's affairs. The fire crew return the tender to its park and remove some of the specialist equipment to lock it away; the accountant and helpers are assessing the results; flight sheets are being completed and any aircraft defects recorded; and when most visitors have left, still there are more than a dozen aeroplanes to wheel back to their beds.

The approach of dusk and an almost deserted grass aerodrome have an irresistible appeal. This is the time to fly, but everyone has worked extremely hard and most are exhausted, so any temptation that creates an extra load on anyone must be dismissed. Soon there will be a flying evening; then a few minutes in the air just before dusk can be enjoyed with a purpose. We must wait, and hope that plenty of visitors will arrive to imbibe the pleasures of such a unique occasion. A daytime display can be great value for participant and onlooker alike; but right at the end of a summer day there can be something even better! Also, an evening event seems to be more enjoyable to organize and to stage . . . so come along and share this special Shuttleworth experience.

9

Old Warden Aerodrome

The grass aerodrome at Old Warden is an exhibit in its own right, for every possible effort has been made to retain a timeless atmosphere appropriate to the type of activity that takes place. Small all-grass aerodromes were commonplace from the start of flight until the forties, when many wartime elementary flying training schools fell into this category. Since then, they have become relative rarities, with the demands of modern aircraft dictating the length and strength of the available runways rather than the number of directions in which taking-off and landing can be carried out. In the thirties, even the major scheduled airline services operated from omni-directional grass airports, but today nearly every such base has become just one long concrete or tarmac strip with no other areas maintained in safe, usable condition. A similar situation applies to many airfields used by the flying Services.

When Richard Shuttleworth obtained his first aeroplane — the Moth G-EBWD — the present site was not suitable to use and he flew from a nearby field on the family estate; but almost immediately he began to prepare his new aerodrome and to do so he needed to remove a number of trees. A story of the time is that his mother, who had no love for aeroplanes, tried very hard to dissuade him, so he encouraged her to take two holidays to the continent. While she was away he organized the felling of trees that would interfere with his flying activities and by the end of her second absence he had achieved his wish. Although apparently annoyed, Mrs Shuttleworth is said to have recognized her son's independence of mind and his determination to fly, so from then on she supported his plans.

Although some sheds had been erected, the first real hangar to be built at Old Warden was the one nearest to the gate from the Biggleswade road; this forms the basis of what is known today as No. 1 hangar. It was developed to include workshops and, later, rooms above, one of which became the drawing office. The stairs for this were made from a section of the main gangway from the *Mauretania* and these remain in use today. The second hangar was constructed during World War II, when the aerodrome was used as a civil-operated servicing base for light types then in military use. All the other hangars have been erected since the war.

During the Richard Shuttleworth era in the thirties, the small aerodrome, with a maximum available length of about 570 yards, had seen many light aircraft types and a number of engineering operations. One of the most

unusual and certainly one of the larger types to appear briefly in 1933 was Blackburn Velos G-AAAW, with its 450 hp Napier Lion engine, a span of forty-eight feet and an all-up weight of 6450 lb. This rare beast, which was a trainer variant of the Blackburn Dart torpedo-bomber, was too thirsty a creature for private operation and soon was dismantled, to provide wood that was used later in restoration of the 1909 Bleriot and 1910 Deperdussin monoplanes.

In an attempt to improve performance and reduce the weight of the rugged Desoutter 1 monoplanes used by Heston-based Warden Aviation, G-AAPZ underwent major surgery at Old Warden. Instrumentation was improved, increased tankage fitted, wheel brakes incorporated and a modified Mk II tail unit installed, but the most drastic modification was replacement of the Cirrus Hermes engine by a Menasco C-4 Pirate. The results, though, were disappointing and subsequent tests proved that the American sales claims could not be matched in practice; the Pirate was unable to deliver its quoted power. Many years later, when other engines from the far side of the Atlantic were proved to be below par on performance, a court case in Britain resulted in a change in the way in which American engine capability and output were published, but the Shuttleworth Desoutter was the first in the line of test cases leading to this move; recently, that Desoutter has been the subject of a detailed restoration project in the capable hands of a small team of volunteers.

In the fifties and early sixties no public displays were staged at Old Warden. The aerodrome was not readily available for general use and in the main the only flying was the occasional test flight or ferry trip to or from a display elsewhere. In 1951 I had a lone first visit when I was asked to collect the 1932 Spartan Arrow G-ABWP, which the Collection had sold for £100 to a private owner at White Waltham. I remember my surprise at the small amount of space available. Fifteen years passed before I saw it again and still there were many operating difficulties, for much of the space that had been used for flying during the war had been returned for agricultural use. Also, hay crops played a revenue-earning role, which for several weeks made taking-off or landing into an increasingly hazardous exercise as each new season matured.

Despite its long history, the Collection was not opened to the general public on a regular basis until 1966, by which time the first Open Days had been established. Usually four or five aeroplanes would be flown before a crowd of a few hundred people, with temporary rope-and-stake barriers erected for each occasion. These were very pleasant informal events, but during preceding years many of the costs of maintaining the aircraft had been covered by covenanted donations from companies within the aircraft industry; now, however, these were ending and clearly some more positive plans were needed to ensure their survival in the longer term.

After the Collection had opened its gates to visitors every day, a shop was established; then a restaurant and snack bar (operated on a franchise basis) were introduced. On the aerodrome, though, much more happened. With such a small site, the management of the time was faced with decisions about how much of the field to keep available for aircraft operations and how much space could safely be made sterile as a car park and viewing enclosure. Maximum availability for flying was achieved by establishing two marked grass runways, but leaving a certain reserve of space for into-wind operation on days on which neither strip could be used safely by the oldest aeroplanes. The public enclosure was erected on a permanent basis, shaped so that the boundaries of the viewing area were almost parallel to the two runways, providing the largest possible frontal area with almost a right-angle bend nearest to the centre of the airfield; this proved popular also with pilots, who could display the typically slow Shuttleworth aeroplanes to maximum effect round the outside of the bend.

Attendance at displays was increasing; and so were the costs of operating the Collection. The home-based historic aeroplanes formed the main base of attraction for visitors to the shows, for such sights could be seen nowhere else in the world, but to maintain a series of events year after year, the organizers needed to inject some other attractions from further afield. Aircraft could appear on timed 'overhead slots' without landing, but the scope of a show could be extended considerably if some of the visiting performers could present their aircraft on the airfield rather than just flying over.

So two main moves were made. For many years an area of ground to the east of the aerodrome had been isolated in the form of an island, bounded by streams on all sides. The surface was rough and the drainage even worse, but the Royal Engineers welcomed the chance of a useful training exercise in re-routing a fast-flowing brook. The section alongside the existing boundary of the airfield was plugged with gravel to allow below-surface water movement to continue, whilst the eastern section was widened and deepened to accept the main stream. A contractor levelled and drained the area needed for a runway extension and a year later the north-west/south-east strip was ready to accept a much wider range of aircraft types.

Although this extension vastly improved the usefulness of the airfield, the lengthening of one strip only generated

Above: A scene in the de Havilland hangar.

a new problem, for with many aircraft types the crosswind limitations would mean that they could operate safely if the wind was close to the heading of the enlarged strip, but not otherwise. Imagine the dilemma of operating a timed display sequence with that background headache! So the next course of action was brought into play; the physical problem was minute compared with the earlier task, but the delays were greater. Although Shuttleworth property, predictably, the land to the south-west of the other grass runway was declared to be the best piece of grazing ground in Bedfordshire. Such was the competition for space between the Trust's aviation and agricultural interests!

Clearly a solution could and would be found. A complicated compromise was agreed, involving occasional winter use of the airfield by the farm sheep, use of the off-runway airfield grass for crop (but not at hay height) and other well-argued points between the parties involved; but it was resolved amicably and eventually the necessary levelling, marking and fencing work was completed to extend the aerodrome to the south-west. Unlike the other, longer strip, this runway was on level ground, with good clear approaches and climb-out paths at each end. This heading is used whenever possible on display days, for it offers good public viewing and is well-placed for access to the visiting aircraft parking areas. However, with so many wind-sensitive aeroplanes participating in an average Shuttleworth show, there are some days on which the north-west/south-east strip must become the active runway.

Today Old Warden aerodrome is physically hemmed-in to prevent much further extension of the total area. However, some ground to the east, near the windsock, remains available for draining and levelling; there is room along the line of hangars for at least two more buildings to be erected in years to come; and, by arrangement with the Shuttleworth Agricultural College, the amount of off-airfield car parking space available is such that even on the busiest display days this has not been packed to its limits. More serious capacity limitations are imposed by the narrow approach road (on which one of its two lanes must be kept clear for use by emergency services) and the cramped feed-in point at the main gate. The former problem is unsurmountable and any alteration to the latter would necessitate the loss of a small section of one runway and a corner of the aircraft parking/manoeuvring area.

Perhaps these small problems represent a form of disguised blessing, for the Shuttleworth Collection and Old Warden Aerodrome combine to make something that is so indescribably different. Many people have expressed their hope that the timeless atmosphere will be retained, that it will not be cheapened by overt commercialism, that the place will not grow into a large and impersonal entity lacking in traditional values. Considerable care has been taken throughout the development stages to ensure that the necessary expansion has been affected with as little change as possible to the overall 'air' that surrounds the Shuttleworth scene.

Clearly, growth must bring some noticeable changes. One change that several visitors have not liked has been the increase in the scale of the flying functions, many of which have expanded from the casual open days of the sixties into full-scale, formal, but still unique flying displays. So in 1982 a fresh policy was introduced. A few major events were planned to cater for the needs of families and large crowds, while several smaller informal occasions were aimed at the more specialist visitors who sought space and freedom with opportunities for photography, filming and sound-recording. Three years previously the Collection had pioneered flying evenings, when some of the earliest of veteran aeroplanes could be demonstrated in the calm conditions that prevail so often in the last hour or two before dusk; these have helped to recreate the informal and unhurried atmosphere that was one of the main features of the first open days. All concerned hope that this revised display pattern can be continued for many years, thereby providing events to suit the needs and interests of every visitor.

Whatever happens elsewhere, Old Warden will remain as a small, all-grass aerodrome with a minimum of hard surface area, in pleasant rural surroundings, to provide a virtual haven for those who wish to be surrounded by some of the best of the past. It is a popular place to visit, not only for those who arrive by road, but for many members of the private flying fraternity who seek somewhere to land that is away from the tarmac-surfaced, radio-cluttered airports and airfields that form the basis of the world of general aviation today. Because of this difference, Old Warden is a much-sought site for various non-Shuttleworth events such as model aeroplane competitions, kite festivals, fly-ins by aviation clubs and associations and occasionally private functions. On some occasions the aerodrome must be closed to all other aircraft, but each event helps to produce revenue for the Collection and on most days in the year the grass is available for all who wish to fly-in to see the historic exhibits or just to relax in the open. Just in case something special is happening, though, prior permission is required and all pilots are asked to remember that Old Warden is a private, unlicensed airfield in a rural area where peace and quiet are appreciated by the Collection's neighbours!

Appendix I
Aircraft not on display

Although a guide of this nature must have an active life of several years, it would be unwise to include detailed references to aircraft or other exhibits that are unlikely to appear on public display during this time. However, the Shuttleworth Collection owns a number of items that are undergoing very long-term restoration or are stored in various places awaiting their turn to enter the workshops. Brief details of the aeroplanes that fall into this group are given here:

BRISTOL M1C: A reproduction of the Bristol M1C is being built for the Collection. A certain mystery surrounds the history of the type. Why was an aeroplane with similar speed and manoeuvrability to the S.E.5a, but which could have been available many months earlier, not ordered in substantial numbers, and indeed why were the few that were produced sent not to the hard pressed squadrons on the Western Front but to the Middle East theatre of the war?

The prototype numbered the Bristol M1A was first flown on 14 July 1916 and was powered by a 110 hp Clerget rotary engine. This was followed by three further machines powered by 110 hp Le Rhône engines, and a fourth initially powered by an AR1 rotary engine, which, according to the drawings was designated a M1C. Although this M1C was produced in March, an order for production aircraft was not placed until the following August, when 125 M1Cs were ordered with 110 Le Rhônes. Although certain internal design changes appear to have been made during the production run the M1C designation was not changed.

Various theories exist over why it was not ordered in numbers, ranging from it having a high landing speed, poor downward visibility, having a short endurance period or pure prejudice against the monoplane format – a throw back to a pre-war monoplane ban. Whatever the reason, the hopes of the pilots on the Western Front were raised by the rumours of the new scout only to fade as the machines failed to appear.

The few that did see service in Palestine and Mesopotamia did well, but many went straight to training depots here and abroad. It is a measure of the machine's popularity that many instructors took over Bristols for their own use, including James McCudden VC and Harold Balfour.

The Bristol M1C forms the second project undertaken by the Northern Aeroplane Workshops, their first being the Sopwith Triplane built for, and now flying with, the Collection. NAW is an amateur organisation whose members meet in their spare time to construct fully airworthy replicas employing original materials and working to the original drawings. When the M1C has been completed, they hope to build a third aeroplane that will be destined to live at Old Warden.

ANEC II: G-EBJO. Built 1924. One of three monoplanes designed by W S Shackleton and constructed at Addlestone, in Surrey, by the Air Navigation and Engineering Company. Designed for an Air Ministry competition for two-seaters; originally powered by an Anzani and later restored with a 32 hp Bristol Cherub. It had five owners, including Norman Jones of Tiger Club renown (1926), Allen Wheeler, a former Shuttleworth Aviation Trustee (1929) and Jimmy Edmunds who passed it to Richard Shuttleworth in 1937. It is a large machine for such low power, with a span of thirty-eight feet and yet an empty weight of only 420 lb. It has been stored at Old Warden since the start of World War II and is in need of a total rebuild.

1930: Blake Bluetit

Acquired 1968

Span: 27 ft 8 in
Empty weight: 460 lb
Power: 35 hp ABC Gnat horizontal twin

The Bluetit was constructed at Kings Worthy, Hampshire, by two young mining engineers, the brothers W H C and R C Blake, during the former's ten-week annual leave in the autumn of 1930. It was an ingenious 'bitza', constructed from surplus aeroplane parts: the wings were cut down from a pair of Avro 504 upper mainplanes bought for £5; the rest was devised around the rear fuselage sections from two Simmonds Spartans, together with one undercarriage and 'universal' tail unit, all acquired for a few shillings. The engine, dating from the 1914-18 war, was obtained in new condition, with a second, damaged one for £6. Apart from untold hours of hard work, the total cost of parts and materials was just £26!

The first ten-minute flight was made on 19 October 1930 by W H C Blake, who flew the aeroplane several times over the next two years. Apart from the unreliability of the engine, the machine behaved very well, despite having been 'designed' more by eye and guesswork than anything else. It was overturned and damaged on the ground by a sudden gale in 1932, after which it was not repaired but stored in a barn on the Blake family farm.

The Exhibit: The Bluetit was never registered and remained in storage at Kings Worthy until being given by W H C Blake to the Collection in July 1968. In 1988, restoration was begun by a team of volunteers from the Shuttleworth Veteran Aeroplane Society.

Appendix II
Markings, Colour Schemes and Dates of Origin

Where practicable, the aeroplanes in the Shuttleworth Collection are presented in colours and markings that are appropriate to their eras. This brief general description may be helpful towards understanding the many variations.

Early Flying Machines: These were finished in a clear dope only to tauten the fabric; colours were not used because of the extra weight. No formal registration markings were carried, but today the survivors have new national identities recorded by the British Aviation Preservation Council, e.g. the Collection's 1910 Deperdussin is listed as BAPC 4. Also, civil registrations have been allocated by the Civil Aviation Authority although these are not carried on the aircraft.

Military aeroplanes: Aircraft were painted in schemes appropriate to their intended duties and areas of operation. In peacetime conditions, a silver finish (natural or painted) has been a standard practice, with, for example, yellow (later dayglo orange) conspicuity-bands on wings and round the fuselages on machines used for training. At some periods, e.g. in the mid thirties and just after World War II, many trainers were painted yellow overall, sometimes, in the first case, with polished silver engine cowlings.

In wartime or with the threat of war, aircraft have been painted in dark colours, such as olive drab in the 1914-18 period; or the lozenge camouflage used by the Germans, which can be seen on the Collection's LVG CVI; World War II saw many schemes, including dark earth and green as a standard camouflage, replaced in some areas by grey and green. For desert operations a lighter sandy brown has been used, while until recently a deepish blue was standard on many high-altitude photographic reconnaissance aircraft.

Although there have been certain exceptions, often for security reasons, generally the serial numbers of Service aeroplanes have been a guide to their age, with consecutive numbers issued for specific production batches. Starting with A1 in 1916, a single letter followed by up to four figures was used until the early part of World War II, by which time all these had been allotted; as an example, K and L prefixes were standard during the thirties, such as L8032 of the Shuttleworth Gladiator of 1938. When two-letter prefixes became necessary, the numbers were reduced to three, e.g. AR 501, which is the Collection's 1941 Spitfire.

Civil Aeroplanes: Colours are largely a matter of owners' personal choice, with private machines painted to individual taste and commercial aircraft to the operators' house schemes. For practical purposes, as far as surviving machines are concerned, (although a temporary scheme from May to July 1919 used the letter K followed by three figures from 100 onwards) all British civil aircraft have a five-letter registration, comprising a G followed by a dash and four letters giving the individual identity. Aircraft registered between July 1919 and 1928 have G-E prefixes (E standing for England, with C used for Canada etc.), but in 1928 this was abandoned by international agreement and the countries in the then British Empire acquired their own lettering. Machines registered in Britain started again at the beginning of the alphabet, i.e. G-AAAA. Examples of both schemes can be found in the Collection, such as the 1928 DH 60X Moth G-EBWD and the 1935 Percival Gull G-ADPR. Today G-B registrations are issued, but now the Civil Aviation Authority will issue out-of-sequence allocations to those who ask, making impossible the task of using the letters as a guide to a machine's year of registration.

Dates of origin: If there is one aspect in the search for historical accuracy that guarantees a headache for an author, the date to quote for a type must take a lead! What is the correct date to use? The year in which design work started or finished, the year in which the prototype (which may have been very different from the later production machine) flew, the time of the type entering service, the year in which the particular mark or variant was introduced or the date on which the exhibit was built?

Consider the Gloster Gladiator: the private-venture prototype Gloster S5.37 flew in September 1934, but was unnamed until the RAF placed an order in July of the following year. The type entered squadron service in February 1937. The Collection's specimen was built-up from two different, but original, airframes in 1938. Although in 1934 there was an aeroplane in existence that today would be called Gladiator, at the time there was no aeroplane with that name, so 1935 seems the year to use.

As a general base, the years used are those in which the standard production versions entered military or civil service, but still there are problems. Design work on the little amateur-built Granger Archaeopteryx began in 1926 and it first flew in 1930, but its identity G-ABXL dates it as 1932, for it was not registered until that year. Only one was constructed, so there cannot be a time of entering service and in this case reference to the year of the first flight gives due credit to the foresight of its designers.

What about the Spitfire? The prototype flew in 1936 and the first Mark Is were delivered to the RAF in 1938; but the Collection's specimen is a mark Vc of 1941, so the date appropriate to the mark (which in fact is the year in which the individual aircraft was built) has been used.

The first Bristol Fighter flew in 1916 and the type went into action in 1917, but the Collection's specimen was not built until the end of the war — in late 1918. However, as it is a standard production machine as built in quantity in the earlier year, common sense seems to say that 'Bristol Fighter 1917' is the most appropriate description.

There are many other anomalies. The problems of dating are as endless as the choices, so perhaps you will accept that while the results in this book may be open to question, they are as accurate as history allows?

* * *

Registrations allocated by the Civil Aviation Authority to aircraft that do not display their civil identities:

Registration	Type	Identity Marks Displayed (if any)
* G-ASPP	Bristol Boxkite	—
G-AWII	Supermarine Spitfire	AR501
G-ANKT	DH-82A Tiger Moth	T6818
G-AOTD	DHC-1 Chipmunk	WB588
* G-ARSG	Avro Triplane	'Avro'
G-EBNV	English Electric Wren	'4'
G-AEPH	Bristol F-2B	D8096
* G-AANI	Blackburn Monoplane	—
* G-AANJ	LVG-CVI	7198/18
G-EBIA	S.E.5A	F904
* G-ACNB (G-ADEV)	Avro 504K	H5199
* G-AJRS	Miles M14A Magister	P6382
* G-AENP	Hawker Hind	K5414
G-AHSA	Avro Tutor	K3215
G-AFTA	Hawker Tomtit	K1786
* G-AANH	Deperdussin Monoplane	—
G-AMRK	Gloster Gladiator	L8032
* G-AANG	Bleriot Monoplane	—
G-EBKY	Sopwith Pup	N6181
G-ASOP	Sopwith Camel	B6219

* *indicates recent CAA allocation and not original registration.*

Appendix III
Information for visitors

Location:

The Shuttleworth Collection is housed at Old Warden Aerodrome, which is two miles west of the A1 trunk road near Biggleswade in Bedfordshire. The nearest railway station is Biggleswade, on the East Coast Main Line, to which fast electric trains run regularly from London King's Cross. Access is possible also from Bedford on the Thameslink route from Brighton, Gatwick, London and Luton, as an occasional United Counties bus service operates between the two stations and passes reasonably close to the aerodrome. Taxis are available at Biggleswade.

Opening:

Except for 10 days at Christmas, the Collection is open to visitors daily from 10 a.m. to 4 p.m. (3 p.m. November to March) — and closes one hour after last admission, or dusk if this is earlier. A gift shop is open at the same times and a restaurant and snack bar are operated by a contractor on a concession basis. There is ample space for picnics in pleasant rural surroundings.

Education facilities:

Facilities are available for parties to be given introductory talks or guided tours; a special leaflet gives details. Advance bookings must be made.

The Collection publishes a number of books and booklets. A companion volume to this guide, *From Bleriot to Spitfire*, describes the handling qualities of many of the historic aeroplanes.

There is a limited library and research facility, for which a charge is made to users. A lecture room may be hired for meetings and conferences.

Lectures on the Collection or on specific aspects of the Collection's activities, e.g. restoration, flying or displays are available to recognized bodies, but requests should be made in writing well in advance of any chosen dates.

Displays:

Flying displays are held regularly between May and September each year and on some occasions the historic vehicles are paraded. Also, functions such as model aircraft competitions, kite festivals and motor rallies take place each summer. A calendar of each season's events is available free of charge on receipt of a stamped addressed envelope. Normally this is published in March.

Charitable status:

The Shuttleworth Trust is a registered charity, number 1012224. Donations should be made payable to the Shuttleworth Collection. Where appropriate, gifts by Deed of Covenant enable the Collection to recover the income tax paid by the donor.

The Swiss Garden

An attractive garden with ponds, paths and bridges is owned by the Shuttleworth Trust, but is leased to Bedfordshire County Council. It adjoins the aerodrome and is open regularly.

Old Warden Aerodrome:

Old Warden is a small, private, unlicensed grass aerodrome. Visitors are welcome to fly-in subject to obtaining prior permission. It is in a quiet farming area and pilots are asked to avoid low flying or any other inconsiderate activity that may disturb the peace of the neighbourhood.

Support:

The Shuttleworth Veteran Aeroplane Society serves as a supporting body to the Collection and members may participate in many ways. Newcomers are welcome and details are available on request.

Accuracy

All information in this book is considered to be accurate at the time of publication in 1994, but neither the Trust nor the Collection can be responsible for any changes that may occur during its period of validity as a guide.

Information:

The address for all communications is:
The Shuttleworth Collection, Old Warden Aerodrome, Biggleswade, Bedfordshire SG18 9ER.
The telephone number is 0767 627288.